COLTER'S HELL
&JACKSON'S HOLE

The Fur Trappers' Exploration of the Yellowstone and Grand Teton Park Region

By Merrill J. Mattes

Regional Historian, National Park Service

W9-CPQ-884

Published by

YELLOWSTONE LIBRARY AND MUSEUM ASSOCIATION

and the

GRAND TETON NATURAL HISTORY ASSOCIATION

in cooperation with

NATIONAL PARK SERVICE
U.S. DEPARTMENT OF THE INTERIOR

Proceeds from
booklets sold by
the Yellowstone
Library and
Museum Association
help the
National Park Service
program of
information and
education at
Yellowstone.

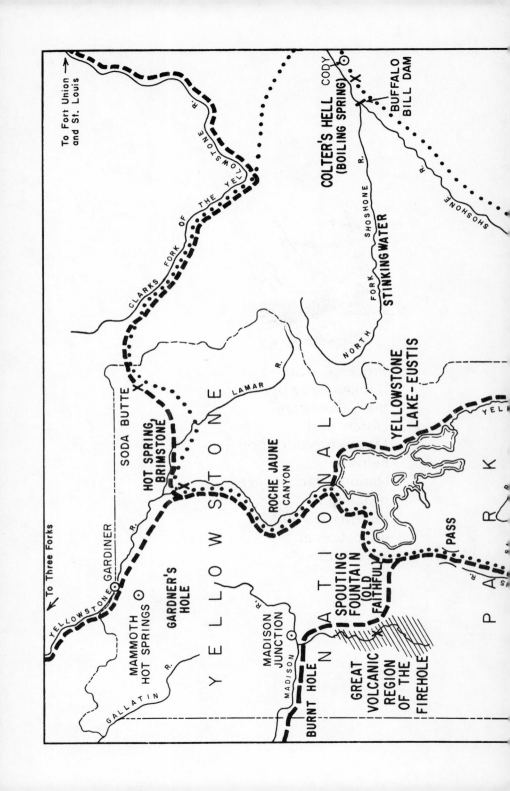

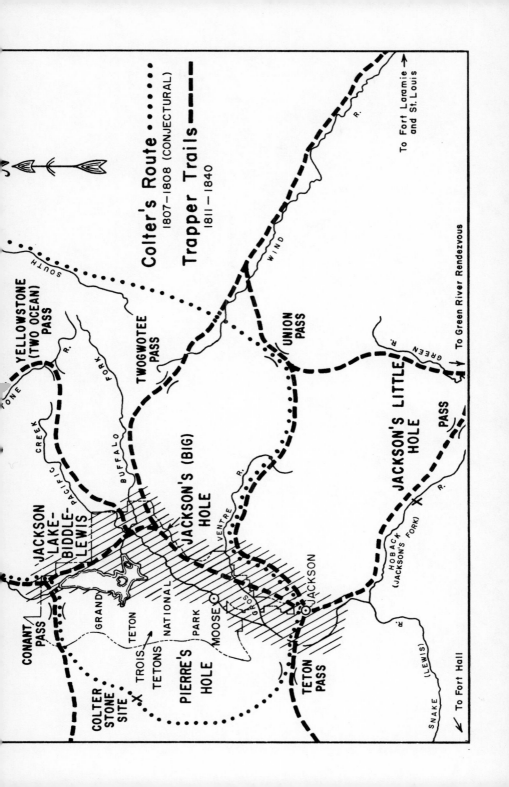

TABLE OF CONTENTS

Page

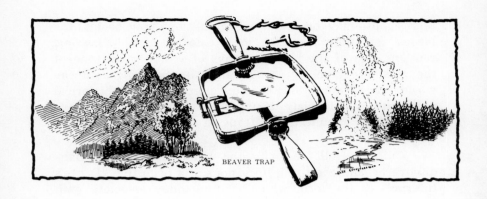

BEAVER TRAP

I. Strange Land of "Volcanoes" and "Shining Mountains"

The Yellowstone-Grand Teton region was not officially discovered and its scenic marvels were not publicly proclaimed until the 1870's, beginning with the Washburn-Langford-Doane expedition. For thirty years before, from 1841 to 1869, this region was a Paradise Lost, rarely visited by white men. But for thirty year before **that,** or from 1807 to 1840, this region had hundreds of appreciative visitors. These were the Rocky Mountain fur trappers. While searching for the golden-brown fur of the beaver, destined for the St. Louis market, these adventurers thoroughly explored this fabulous region. Although news of their discoveries received scant public notice back in the settlements, or was discounted as tall tales, to them belongs the honor of being the first actual explorers of these twin parks.

Neighboring Yellowstone and Grand Teton, established as National Parks in 1872 and 1929, respectively, are separately managed today as units of our National Park System. But geographically, now as well as in the early nineteenth century, they embrace one unique region, characterized by topographic and geologic features that are the crescendo of a great scenic symphony. Here, at the heart of the continent, the source of the three major river systems of the continent—the Columbia, the Colorado, and the Missouri-

Mississippi—may be found the greatest geyser basins, the largest mountain lake, the most colorful of kaleidoscopic canyons, one of the richest arrays of wildlife, and one of the most spectacularly beautiful mountain ranges in the world. The Yellowstone-Grand Teton region has historical unity, also, particularly during the obscure but heroic age of the Rocky Mountain fur trade.

"Colter's Hell"—bearing the name of the legendary discoverer, and conjuring up visions of a primitive "Dante's Inferno"—is the term which visitors today associate with the early history of Yellowstone National Park and its universally famous hydrothermal wonders. Actually, the wandering, bearded, buck-skinned beaver trappers never referred to the geyser region of the upper Madison as Colter's Hell. As we will see, the real Colter's Hell in Jim Bridger's day was another place altogether, having nothing to do with anything within Yellowstone Park itself. In trapper times the Yellowstone geyser area had no fixed name but was variously described by them as a region of "great volcanoes," "boiling springs" or "spouting fountains." On the recently discovered Hood and Ferris maps (see below) it is labeled "the Burnt Hole" (although this name seems to have been restricted by Russell and others to the Hebgen Lake Valley). Captain Bonneville tells us that his men knew of this region as "the Firehole" and this name, as applied to the river draining the geyser basins, survives today.

Yellowstone Park, carved out of territorial Wyoming, Montana, and Idaho, is a rough-edged rectangle of 3,500 square miles that straddles the twisting course of the Continental Divide. It is a geological circus, a unique creation of ancient volcanoes and glaciers, flanked on the southeast and east by the Absaroka Range, on the north by the Snowy Range, on the northwest by the Gallatin and Madison ranges, on the west by the Centennial Range, and on the south by the Teton Mountains.

From the Park flow the headwaters of two continental rivers and their major tributaries. From here the Snake

Indians at Jackson Lake.

River arcs southward toward Jackson's Hole and the cathedral-like Tetons, destined to join the Columbia River and the Pacific Ocean. Here the Firehole and Gibbon rivers, draining the principal geyser basins, unite to become the Madison River, and here also arises the Gallatin, these being two of the Three Forks of the Missouri. Here arises a branch of the North Fork of the Shoshone River, a tributary of the Bighorn. And here, after its birth near Two Ocean Pass, begins the mighty Yellowstone River which, after passing through its vast mirror-like lake and its prismatic canyon, flows out onto the plains to receive the Bighorn and join the Missouri on its marathon journey to the Mississippi River and the Gulf of Mexico.

This region held a fortune in coveted beaver skins, but it was remote, snowbound, haunted by the vindictive Blackfeet, and plagued by weird visions, sulphurous fumes, and uncanny noises. Here indeed was fertile soil for a legend.

On a clear day Yellowstone Park visitors can see to the south the mountain spires which identify Grand Teton National Park of Wyoming, an indefinable shape of 500 square miles. (The actual boundaries of these neighboring parks are separated by a scant five miles.) The Tetons are perhaps the most distinctive of the granite giants which comprise the Rocky Mountains. A series of sharp pyramids of naked rock, the peaks stand like sharks' teeth against the sky. The most precipitous sides and the most needle-like summit belong to the highest of these, the Grand Teton, which rises over 7,000 feet from its immediate base, nearly 14,000 feet above the level of the distant sea.

The Teton Mountains are the most conspicuous landmarks of a region which contains the scrambled sources of the three greatest river systems of continental United States. As we have seen, Yellowstone Park to the north gives birth to the eastward-flowing Missouri and the westward flowing Columbia waters. East of the Tetons, in the Wind River Mountains, is the head of Green River which rolls southward to merge into the mighty Colorado River, tumbling through the arid lands to the Gulf of California.

Jackson's Hole is that part of the Upper Snake River Valley which lies at the eastern base of the Teton Range. One of the largest enclosed valleys in the Rocky Mountains, its glaciated floor extends about sixty miles north and south, and varies up to twelve miles in width. It is bounded on the west by the Tetons, on the east and south by the less pretentious Mount Leidy Highlands and the Gros Ventre and Hoback Mountains. The Gros Ventres merge imperceptibly into the Wind River Mountains farther east, the crest of which forms the Continental Divide. The southern extremity of the Tetons merges with the eastern end of the Snake River Range near the canyon where the Snake River escapes from the valley.

Historic Jackson's Hole, also known as "Jackson's Big Hole"—but now politely refined to just plain Jackson Hole—was named in 1829 for David Jackson, one of the partners of the Rocky Mountain Fur Company. To the early trapper a "hole" was a sizeable valley abounding in game, and usually (with the exception of Yellowstone's "Firehole") associated with some distinctive personality—hence Brown's Hole, Pierre's Hole, Gardner's Hole, etc. However, Jack-

4

son's Hole was more than just a pleasant spot for trapping and camping. Research gives substance to the view that this was the historic crossroads of the Rocky Mountain fur trade.

Jackson's Hole was destined by geography to become a traffic center of the Western fur trade. Between South Pass at the head of the Little Sandy and the northern passes above the Three Forks of the Missouri it offered the most feasible route across the Rocky Mountain barrier. In addition, it was the focal point of a region that was highly prized and vigorously contested because of its populous beaver streams. Here trappers' trails converged like the spokes of a great wheel and, after Lewis and Clark, most of the important trapper-explorers crossed Jackson's Hole on their journeys.

In historic times there were seven gateways to and from Jackson's Hole: northward up Snake River; northeastward up Pacific Creek to Two Ocean Pass; eastward up Buffalo Fork to Twogwotee Pass; eastward up the Gros

Indian "Buffalo Jump"—Yellowstone Valley.

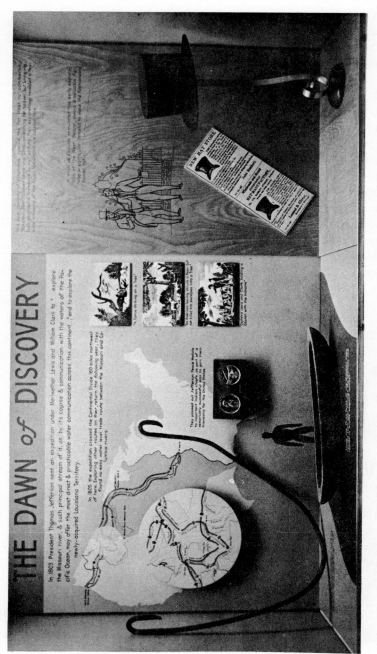

"Dawn of Discovery"—Exhibit in Fur Trade Museum, Grand Teton National Park.

6

Ventre to Union Pass; southward up the Hoback to Green River; westward via Teton Pass or Conant Pass (at the south and north extremities of the Teton Range) to Pierre's Hole.

The Tetons received their name from French-Canadian trappers who accompanied the earliest British expeditions into this territory. As they approached the range from the west, they beheld three towering mountains upon which they bestowed the name of "Trois Tetons" ("Three Breasts"). This romantic designation was readily adopted by the lonely trapping fraternity to whom the sharp snowy peaks (now known as the Grand, Middle and South Tetons) became a beacon to guide them through the hostile wilderness. To the Indians the Tetons were variously known as "The Three Brothers," "The Hoaryheaded Fathers," and "Tee Win-at," meaning "The Pinnacles." The earliest Americans in the region, being more practical than romantic, could find no better name for the silvery spires than "The Pilot Knobs," while an official Hudson's Bay Company map indicates with equal homeliness, "The Three Paps." The name "Three Tetons" survived, however, and was officially recognized by cartographers. The name first appeared publicly in the Bonneville Map of 1837.

The Upper Snake River (i.e., above the mouth of Henry's Fork) was called "Mad River" by the Astorians. Others simply referred to it as the "Columbia River" or "the headwaters of the Columbia," but to most of the fur trappers it was "Lewis River" or "Lewis Fork," so originally named in the Clark Map of 1810 for Capt. Meriwether Lewis, as Clark's Fork of the Columbia was named after his fellow explorer, Capt. William Clark. This name was much more appropriate than its present one, which is derived from the Snake or Shoshone Indians, and first appears on the Greenhow Map of 1840.

In spite of past efforts by water power advocates to "improve" it by a dam, Yellowstone Lake remains just as it was when first discovered by John Colter, the original "Lake Eustis" of the Clark Map of 1810. Jackson Lake,

7

however, was enlarged by a dam built in 1916 by the Bureau of Reclamation. This lake is identifiable with the "Lake Biddle" of the Clark Map of 1810, the "Teton Lake" of Warren A. Ferris, and the "Lewis Lake" referred to frequently by another trapper, Joseph L. Meek. There is today a tributary of the Upper Snake known as Lewis River, heading in a Lewis Lake within the confines of Yellowstone National Park, neither of which are to be confused with the historic "Lewis River" and "Lewis Lake."

Grand Canyon of the Yellowstone.

POWDER HORN

II. The Mystery of "La Roche Jaune" or Yellow Rock River

For some twenty years before the advent of Lewis and Clark, French-Canadian voyageurs of the North West Company were in league with the Mandans, and from these Indians learned of the distant "Pierre Jaune" or "Roche Jaune" River, a translation from the Indian equivalent of "Yellow Rock River." Chittenden theorizes that the ultimate origin of the name descends from the brilliant and infinite varieties of yellow which dominate the color scheme of the Grand Canyon of the Yellowstone, and which probably awed the first aboriginal explorer just as it does today's auto-borne tourist.

Although there is room for debate as to whether any of the Canadian traders beat Lewis and Clark to the mouth of the Yellowstone, it is certain that one of their number preceded the Americans in the approach to its headwaters. On September 10, 1805, Francois Antoine Larocque reached "Riviere aux Roches Jaunes" just below the mouth of Pryor's Fork, near present Billings, Montana, in the course of "a voyage of discovery to the Rocky Mountains." After wintering at the Mandan villages in 1804-1805 as a neighbor of the hibernating Lewis and Clark, and being thwarted in his desire to accompany them upstream, Larocque had returned to his post on the Assiniboine for supplies, then hurried back to the Mandans, going from there overland via Knife River, the Little Missouri, and the Tongue to the Bighorn Mountains, country of the Crows.

While wintering with the Mandans, Captain Clark sketched two maps of the unexplored country westward, based on "the information of traders, indians and my own observation and ideas." One of these shows "Rochejhone River" with six tributaries from the south, five with Indian names, two translated as "Tongue River" and "Big Horn R." The Bighorns and Rocky Mountains beyond are represented only by diagrammatic strokes. There is a trail from the mouth of Knife River to the Bighorns, roughly the same subsequently taken by Larocque. This was actually a refinement of a sketch made for Clark by the Mandan Chief Big White. The second map shows "River yellow rock" minus tributaries but with the Crows ("gens de Corbeau") located just west of an imaginative "montagne de roche—conjecturall." These maps, the first to our knowledge to depict the Yellowstone River, were sent to President Jefferson on April 7, 1805, by Meriwether Lewis, to accompany his eagerly awaited progress report.

Upon their return trip in 1806, after wintering at Fort Clatsop at the mouth of the Columbia, Lewis and Clark divided in order to explore the country more thoroughly, the latter undertaking to determine the source of the mysterious Yellowstone. On July 15, with eleven white men, the Indian woman Sacajawea and her baby, the cavalcade crossed Bozeman Pass, which marks the divide between the Yellowstone and Gallatin Fork, and reached the vicinity of present Livingston, Montana. Never suspecting what wonders lay concealed behind the snowy mountain wall to the south, Clark hurried on down the river to rejoin Lewis, with glory enough for one expedition.

There is only one hint of volcanic phenomena which Clark seems to have obtained from any source other than the presumed conversation with Colter, mentioned below. This was an Indian tale, received after Clark's return, but before Colter's return, to the effect that at the head of Tongue River, a branch of the Yellowstone, "there is frequently heard a loud noise like Thunder, which makes the earth Tremble, they state that they seldom go there because their children Cannot sleep—and Conceive it possessed of spirits, who were averse that men Should be near them." Speculates Vinton, "it can hardly be doubted that the Indians referred to the geyser basin in the Park," rather than to the Tongue River neighborhood.

It is commonly supposed that, prior to Colter, no white man had knowledge of strange phenomena on the Upper Yellowstone, this supposition being one of the pillars of the "first-discovery" theory. It is fairly evident that Clark knew nothing of geysers when he was within seventy-five miles of them in 1806 but, ironically enough, at this time some intimation of them had certainly reached others, including Clark's sponsor, Thomas Jefferson. On October 22, 1805, James Wilkinson, governor of Louisiana Territory, with headquarters in St. Louis, sent to the President, in care of Captain Amos Stoddard,

> a Savage delineation on a Buffalo Pelt, of the Missouri & its South Western branches, including the Rivers plate & Lycorne or Pierre jaune; This Rude Sketch without Scale or Compass 'et remplie de Fantaisies ridicules' is not destitute of Interests, as it exposes the location of several important Objects, & may point the way to useful enquiry— among other things a little incredible, **a volcano is distinctly described on Yellow Stone River.**

Wilkinson apparently obtained this primitive map from unidentified traders. It could not have been a copy of Clark's map sent from Fort Mandan the April previous, for it obviously contained new data. In an advice to Henry Dearborn, Secretary of War, dated September 18, 1805, Wilkinson revealed that his interest in Yellowstone curiosities was sufficiently aroused to dispatch an expedition of his own upriver!

> I have equipt a Perogue out of my Small private means, not with any view to Self interest, to ascend the missouri and enter the River Piere jaune, or yellow Stone, called by the natives, Unicorn River, the same by which

Capt. Lewis I find since expects to return **and which my informants tell me is filled with wonders,** This Party will not get back before the Summer 1807—they are natives of this town. . . .

Who were Wilkinson's explorers, and what became of them? Who were the "informants"? Was their information first-hand or derived from Indians who, unlike the Mandans, were acquainted with details of the Upper Yellowstone? These questions may be unanswerable, but they arise to shadow the giant figure of John Colter.

Fur Trade Museum, Moose Visitor Center—Grand Teton National Park Headquarters.

ing of ourselves *less*. They are self-forgetful. Paul said, *"Forget your-selves long enough to lend a helping hand"* (Philippians 2:4 Msg). This is what it means to "lose your life"—forgetting yourself in service to others. When we stop focusing on our own needs, we become aware of the needs around us.

To be a servant requires a mental shift, a change in your attitudes. God is always more interested in *why* we do something than in what we do. Attitudes count more than achievements. King Amaziah lost God's favor because "*he did what was right in the sight of the LORD, yet not with a true heart*" (2 Chronicles 25:2 **NRSV**).

Servants think more about others than about themselves. Servants focus on others, not themselves. This is true humility: not thinking less of ourselves but think-

HAWKEN RIFLE

III. John Colter, the Phantom Explorer—
1807-1808

The epic journey of discovery known as "The Lewis and Clark Expedition" was organized in the autumn of 1803 at Maysville, Kentucky. Here, on October 15, John Colter enlisted as a private with the stipulated pay of $5 a month, apparently answering the requirement for "good hunters, stout, healthy, unmarried men, accustomed to the woods and capable of bearing bodily fatigue in a pretty considerable degree."

Colter shared all the hardships and triumphs of the expedition, as well as routine adventure in hunting, starving, Indian diplomacy, and getting chased by grizzly bears. In August 1806 the returning party reached the Mandan villages. Here Colter was granted permission by the explorers to take his leave and join two trappers from Illinois, Forrest Hancock and Joseph Dickson, bound for Yellowstone River.

The extent of the wanderings of this trio is not known. In the spring of 1807 Colter alone paddled a canoe down the Missouri to the mouth of the Platte where he found keel-boats of the Missouri Fur Company of St. Louis, led by Manuel Lisa. He was promptly recruited and went with this expedition up the Missouri and the Yellowstone to the mouth of the Bighorn River, where Lisa built a log fort known as Fort Raymond or Manuel's Fort.

It was from this point that Colter made his famous journey of discovery during the autumn and winter of 1807-1808. Colter left no written record of his own. The only thing resembling written evidence is the following by Henry Brackenridge, who heard it from Manuel Lisa:

> He [Lisa] continued his voyage to the Yellowstone River, where he built a trading fort. He shortly after dispatched Coulter, the hunter before mentioned, to bring some of the Indian nations to trade. This man, with a pack of thirty pounds weight, his gun and some ammunition, went upwards of five hundred miles to the Crow nation; gave them information, and proceeded from them to several other tribes. On his return, a party of Indians in whose company he happened to be was attacked, and he was lamed by a severe wound in the leg; notwithstanding which, he returned to the establishment, entirely alone and without assistance, several hundred miles.

Aside from this slim clue, his course can be determined solely on the basis of "Colter's Route in 1807" and other data which appear on William Clark's "Map of the West," published in 1814, presumably based on a conversation of 1810 at St. Louis, whither the trapper-explorer returned after hair-raising adventures with the Blackfeet in the Three Forks country. Inevitably, in view of the topographical errors and distortions of the Clark map, Colter's precise route is subject to wide differences of opinion.

A composite of theories offered by Hiram M. Chittenden, Stallo Vinton, Charles Lindsay, and Burton Harris, to mention only four qualified scholars who have undertaken to hypothecate Colter's route, is that Colter ascended the Bighorn, followed up the Shoshone River to near present Cody, went south along the foot of the Absaroka Mountains, up Wind River to Union Pass, into Jackson's Hole, thence probably across Teton Pass into Pierre's Hole, thence north via Conant Pass to the the west shore of Yellowstone Lake and northeast to the crossing of the Yellowstone near Tower Falls, thence up the Lamar River and Soda Butte Creek, back across the Absarokas, thence south to the Shoshone River, and back to Lisa's Fort by way of Clark's Fork and Pryor's Fork.

The key to Colter's route is the identification of Lakes Jackson and Yellowstone, respectively, as Clark's Lake Biddle (named for the patron of his publication) and Lake Eustis (named for the Secretary of War), no longer questioned by historians. The "Hot Spring Brimstone" at the sulphur beds crossing of the Yellowstone River near Tower Falls and the "Boiling Spring" near the forks of the Stinkingwater or Shoshone (see Chapter IV) are other checkpoints which now seem quite firm. In addition, there are two interesting claims of physical evidence. While these are both necessarily debatable and subject to challenge as hoaxes, they deserve consideration. According to Philip A. Rollins, quoted by Vinton:

> In September of 1889, Tazewell Woody (Theodore Roosevelt's hunting guide), John H. Dewing (also a hunting guide) and I, found on the left side of Coulter Creek, some fifty feet from the water and about three quarters of a mile above the creek's mouth, a large pine tree on which was a deeply indented blaze, which after being cleared of sap and loose bark was found to consist of a cross thus 'X' (some five inches in height), and, under it, the initials 'J C' (each some four inches in height).
>
> The blaze appeared to these trained hunting guides, so they stated to me, to be approximately eighty years old.
>
> They refused to fell the tree and so obtain the exact age of the blaze because they said they guessed the blaze had been made by Colter himself.
>
> The find was reported to the Government authorities, and the tree was cut down by them in 1889 or 1890, in order that the blazed section might be installed in a museum, but as I was told in the autumn of 1890 by the then superintendent of the Yellowstone Park, the blazed section had been lost in transit.

The second reputed Colter relic, which has survived, is the so-called "Colter Stone" which is now exhibited by the National Park Service in its new Fur Trade Museum at the Moose Visitor Center, Grand Teton National Park. This is a piece of rhyolite hand-carved roughly in the shape of a

Colter's Hell today (with Superintendent Lon Garrison and wife).
Photo by Author

human head, with the inscribed lettering "John Colter 1808." This specimen was dug up in 1931 by William Beard and son while clearing timber on their farm about five miles east of Tetonia, Idaho, just within the Wyoming state line. In 1933 Aubrey Lyon, a neighbor, obtained the "stone head" in trade for a pair of riding boots, and presented it to park officials.

Although the natural tendency to view such finds with skepticism may be respected here, several factors lend plausibility. Members of the Beard family had no knowledge of John Colter. In 1931 the Colter story had not been well researched, and the version then was largely confined to the year 1807; yet if Colter made winter camp in the Teton Basin, and left a record to help while away the time, this would logically occur early in 1808. The stone itself yields no conclusive evidence on the basis of wear or patination; but some geologists agree that 125 years of weathering and soil acidity could have elapsed between the initial carving and time of discovery. At least the Colter Stone is a great historical conversation piece!

According to Thomas James, an associate of Colter's, the fight with the Blackfeet, mentioned by Brackenridge as occurring on Colter's Yellowstone journey, did not actually occur until the summer of 1808, near the Three Forks of the Missouri. On this occasion Colter was wounded in the furious battle between the Blackfeet and Flatheads.

Still later in 1808 Colter and John Potts (another Lewis and Clark veteran) were captured by Blackfeet on Jefferson River. Potts was killed and dismembered. Colter was stripped naked and told to run for his life. The Indians, who were to have great sport with Colter in this way, were enraged when he managed to escape his tormentors and kill one of them. He finally made his way back to Manuel's Fort, greatly emaciated.

After this fabulous feat of endurance, Colter remained in the wilderness until 1810, when he guided Colonel Menard to Three Forks, where a new fort was built, which was subject to constant Blackfeet harassment. Vowing never to return to the mountains, Colter returned downriver to St. Louis, arriving in May 1810 after six years of perils which well entitle him to claim as "The American Ulysses."

Colter settled at the village of Charette, a few miles above the mouth of the Missouri River, and married a girl named Sally. According to Washington Irving, in 1811 Wilson Price Hunt of the Astorian expedition attempted to persuade Colter to join him but this Colter declined to do after "balancing the charms of his bride against those of the Rocky Mountains." In 1813 he died, ingloriously, of "jaundice." Thus passed the phantom discoverer of the Teton-Yelowstone region, to whom James pays this tribute:

> [Colter was] five feet ten inches in height and wore an open, ingenious ,and pleasing countenance of the Daniel Boone stamp. Nature had formed him, like Boone, for hardy indurance of fatigue, privation and perils . . . His veracity was never questioned among us and his character was that of a true American backwoodsman.

Upper Geyser Basin from the cone of Old Faithful. W. H. Jackson photo, 1871

18

WHISKEY KEGS

IV. "Colter's Hell": A Case of Mistaken Identity

One of the most venerable old axioms of fur trade history is that of Colter's Hell, which may be formulated thus: "After John Colter discovered what is now Yellowstone National Park, he told others of the scenic wonders there. No one believed him, and his listeners derisively dubbed the imaginary place Colter's Hell." No item of Yellowstone history is more widely believed, more universally beloved, and more transparently incorrect.

There **was** a Colter's Hell in the fur trappers lexicon, which referred specifically to an ancient thermal area bordering the Shoshone River just west of present Cody, Wyoming. The term was **never** applied historically to the thermal zone within Yellowstone Park itself. It was Hiram M. Chittenden, the esteemed engineer and historian who first suggested this usage in 1895 with the original edition of his book, **Yellowstone National Park.**

The earliest published reference to "Colter's Hell" is in Washington Irving's version of Capt. Benjamin L. E. Bonneville's journal narrating events from 1832 to 1835. However, note here that this "volcanic tract" with its "gloomy terrors, its hidden fires, smoking pits, noxious streams and the all-pervading 'smell of brimstone'" was located, according to Irving, not on the headwaters of the Yellowstone but on the Shoshone or "the Stinking River" or "the Stinking-water," originally named on the Clark Map. It was Chittenden in 1895 and not Irving in 1837 who started the legend by asserting vaguely that "the region of . . . [Colter's] adventures was long derisively known as 'Colter's Hell,'" implying that by "region" he meant Yellowstone Park, the subject of his book. He does not accuse Bonneville or Irving of error, perforce conceding that "this name early came to be restricted to the locality where Colter discovered the tar spring on the Stinkingwater," but he hopefully guesses that "Colter's description, so well summed up by Irving . . . undoubtedly referred in large part to what he saw in the Yellowstone and Snake River Valleys." This is where the misconception got started.

It is significant that no historian prior to Chittenden entertained this misconception. For example, in 1890 Hubert H. Bancroft wrote: "Far east of . . . [the volcanic basins on the Upper Madison], on the Stinkingwater Fork . . . is Colter's Hell, where similar phenomenon is exhibited on a lesser scale." It is further significant that in his monumental **American Fur Trade of the Far West,** the first edition of which appeared in 1902, seven years after the first edition of **Yellowstone,** Chittenden wrote that Colter was "the first to pass through the singular region which has since become known throughout the world as the Yellowstone Wonderland. He **also** saw the immense tar spring at the forks of Stinkingwater River, a spot which came to bear the name of Colter's Hell." This is his only reference here to the term, which is a clear if tacit admission that he was in error in the first instance to create the impression that it ever applied contemporaneously to Yellowstone Park. But the impression once created would not down. Like Aladdin's wonderful lamp, the jinni was out of the bottle, and the poetic version of "Colter's Hell" has become a stock item in Western literature.

Defenders of the Colter's Hell mythology are eager to challenge Washington Irving as an authority. True, Irving's

Colter Monument.

Captain Bonneville by his own admission never personally saw the Yellowstone Park area. Also, it is true that geysers are not to be seen today along the Shoshone River. Hence it might be reasoned that the only noteworthy thermal activity in 1807 was likewise confined to the Yellowstone (more particularly, to the upper Madison), and that Bonneville was merely reporting a twisted rumor. But a cold examination of the facts shows that Irving and Bonneville were correct.

First, there is no good reason to question Bonneville's geographical knowledge. While he never saw it himself, Bonneville had quite a crew circulating through the future park as early as 1833 and, in fact, there is reason to believe that the great geyser basin of Firehole River, climaxed by Old Faithful, was discovered that year by one of his own lieutenants (see Chapter VII).

Secondly, although there are no phenomena readily apparent to passing motorists at the bona fide and unmarked Colter's Hell site just west of Cody, the evidence of thermal activity, not entirely extinct now, is abundantly evident to

Colter Stone Find Site (Wyoming).

Photo by Author

anyone who cares to pause enroute to or from Yellowstone's East Gate. On the Canyon rim downstream from the rocky defile enclosing the Buffalo Bill Dam, there are extinct geyser cones up to thirty feet in height and an extensive crust of fragile sinter. In the canyon floor itself there are bubbling fountains in the river bed, and the same pervasive smell of rotten eggs, (or more scientifically, sulphur dioxide) which assails one's nostrils on the Upper Firehole. (Other related hot springs once existed at the forks of the Shoshone, now drowned beneath the reservoir).

How very strange that this spot, quite evidently the "Boiling Spring" of Colter's famous route on the William Clark Map of 1810, has been largely ignored since 1895. Campfire writers and lecturers have been so enchanted by the Yellowstone "Wonderland," they never gave thought to this historical-geological feature 50 miles outside of the Park boundary.

Thirdly, Bonneville wasn't the only one who knew about the phenomena on the Stinkingwater. The true identity of Colter's Hell was well understood by other mountain men. In 1829 Joe Meek knew all about steam vents "on the Yellowstone Plains," but he also was familiar with a volcanic tract on "Stinking Fork," previously "seen by one of Lewis and Clarke's men, named Colter, while on a solitary hunt, and by him also denominated 'hell.' " In 1852 the famed missionary-explorer, Father De Smet, cited "Captain Bridger" as the source of his information that, "Near the source of the River Puante, which empties into the Big Horn . . . is a place called Colter's Hell—from a beaver-hunter of that name. This locality is often agitated with subterranean fires . . ."

Stallo Vinton, early Colter biographer and editor of the 1935 edition of Chittenden's **American Fur Trade,** paid no attention to Chittenden's footnoted correction of 1902. Rather, he did more than anyone, perhaps, to exterminate the true Colter's Hell and pin the name on the National Park. He accuses Irving of a substantial error in locating "Hell" on the Stinking River. Similarly, he ignores Joe Meek's careful distinction between the Yellowstone and Shoshone volcanic tracts.

In 1863 Walter Washington DeLacy accompanied a party of Montana gold-seekers through the Yellowstone Park area. Although his companions were too absorbed in the search for the precious metal to pay any attention to the scenic wonders, DeLacy, a surveyor by trade, did pay attention and subsequently published a crude but illuminating map of the Park region. Here the principal geyser basin on Firehole River is called "Hot Springs Valley." And far to the east, near the forks of the Shoshone is a "Hot Spring, Colter's Hill." [sic] In 1867 the official map of the Interior Department, by Keeler, apparently reproducing DeLacy's data, also indicates a "Hot Spring, Coulter's Hill." [sic] So the Federal Government, at this early date, gave this official recognition to the clear distinction between the two thermal areas.

Vinton refers to the DeLacy and Keeler maps but he dismisses this further evidence as a mistake. Perhaps his

23

stubborn version of Colter's Hell would have collapsed if he had seen the recently discovered Bridger-DeSmet Map of 1851, in the Office of Indian Affairs. Here Bridger also clearly distinguishes between "Sulphur Spring or Colter's Hell Volcano" on Stinking Fork and an entirely different "Great Volcanic Region in state of eruption" drained by Firehole River. (See Chapter VIII.) Can we invoke any higher authority than Jim Bridger?

Jim Bridger.

GREEN RIVER KNIFE

V. "Les Trois Tetons": The Golden Age of Discovery, 1810-1824

In the spring of 1810, after Colter had departed, the Missouri Fur Company fort at Three Forks was so besieged by the Blackfeet that Andrew Henry was forced to flee with his trappers southwestward. They crossed the Continental Divide to the north fork of Snake River, since known as Henry's Fork. A few log shelters built here near present St. Anthony, Idaho, called "Henry's Fort," became the first American establishment on the Pacific slope. During the rigorous winter of 1810-1811 it may be reasoned that these men explored the country within a wide radius of the Teton Mountains. Any belief that they touched Yellowstone Park must be conjectural, but that they were acquainted with Jackson's Hole is quite evident from the testimony of the Astorians. In the spring of 1811 the starving company disbanded. Henry and others returned down the Missouri via Three Forks, while John Hoback, John Robinson and Jacob Reznor went eastward via Teton Pass, Jackson's Hole, Twogwotee Pass, and overland to the Arikara villages on the Missouri, where they shaped a dugout and proceeded downstream.

In 1808 John Jacob Astor secured a charter from the state of New York creating the American Fur Company. The most ambitious of his schemes was the establishment of a trading post at the mouth of the Columbia River, to exploit the wealth of the Northwestern wilderness. To promote this enterprise, Astor organized the subsidiary Pacific Fur Company and sent out two expeditions, one of which went by sea around Cape Horn, while the other was to proceed overland along the route of Lewis and Clark. The overland Astorians achieved fame as the first transcontinental expedition after Lewis and Clark, but fate decreed that they should blaze their own trail—through Jackson's Hole.

Early in 1811 the overland party, under the command of Wilson Price Hunt of New Jersey, left St. Louis and sailed by keelboat up the Missouri River. On May 26, near the mouth of the Niobrara River, they met Hoback, Robinson, and Reznor. This trio was persuaded to join the outfit as guides and hunters, and it appears that it was their reports of hostile Indians on the Upper Missouri that prompted Hunt to abandon his boats on July 18 at the Arikara villages and proceed on dry land. From this point on the expedition consisted of 82 horses, 62 men, and the squaw and two children belonging to the interpreter Pierre Dorion.

Fort Astoria.

26

The hopeful caravan retraced the route that Hoback and his companions had followed across the trackless plains and the Bighorn Mountains, then started up Wind River. Here, on September 14, according to Irving's **Astoria**, the guides

> assured Mr. Hunt that, by following up Wind River, and crossing a single mountain ridge, he would come upon the head waters of the Columbia. The scarcity of game, however, which already had been felt to a pinching degree, and which threatened them, with famine among the sterile heights which lay before them, admonished them to change their course. It was determined, therefore, to make for a stream [Green River] which, they were informed, passed the neighboring mountains to the south of west, on the grassy banks of which it was probable they would meet with buffalo. Accordingly about three o'clock on the following day, meeting with a beaten Indian road which led in the proper direction, they struck into it, turning their backs upon Wind River.
>
> In the course of the day they came to a height that commanded an almost boundless prospect. Here one of the guides paused, and, after considering the vast landscape attentively, pointed to three mountain peaks glistening with snow [the Tetons], which rose, he said, above a fork of Columbia River. They were hailed by the travellers with that joy with which a beacon on a sea-shore is hailed by mariners after a long and dangerous voyage. . . .

After a buffalo hunt on the "Spanish" or Green River, the Astorians crossed the dividing ridge to the head of the Hoback River (presumably then named in honor of their guide), which they followed into Jackson's Hole.

The Hunt cavalcade paused at the confluence of the Hoback and the Snake rivers, and debated. "Should they abandon their horses, cast themselves loose in fragile barks upon this wild, doubtful, and unknown river; or should they continue their more toilsome and tedious, but perhaps more certain wayfaring by land?" After some tentative exploring of the Snake River Canyon, and upon the advice of the three hunters, they wisely decided in favor of the latter course. They forded the Snake, and on October 5 as they crossed "the mountain [Teton Pass] . . . by an easy and well-beaten trail, snow whitened the summit. . . ." On the 8th they arrived at Andrew Henry's abandoned post. Here Hoback, Robinson, Reznor, and two others left the party on a separate exploring trip; and here it was that Hunt yielded to the demands of his followers, which he previously had resisted, and abandoned his horses in favor of passage by canoe flotilla down the Snake, a tragic mistake which brought great suffering to the Astorians before they reached their goal.

While the main body passed on, four men remained in Jackson's Hole to "catch beaver." This was the first known actual trapping of that area. Even more important, it was the first actual step in the great commercial project of Astoria. Irving recognized the significance of this move:

> [The expedition] had now arrived at the head waters of the Columbia, which were among the main points embraced by the enterprise of Mr. Astor. These upper streams were reputed to abound in beaver, and had as yet been unmolested by the white trapper. The numerous signs of beaver met with during the recent search for timber gave evidence that the neighborhood was a good 'trapping ground.' Here then it was proper to begin to cast loose those leashes of hardy trappers, that are detached from trading parties, in the very heart of the wilderness. The men detached in the present instance were Alexander Carson, Louis St. Michel, Pierre Detaye, and Pierre Delaunay.

Snake River crossing.

Photo by Author

28

These men were instructed to "trap upon the upper part of Mad (Snake) River, and upon the neighboring streams." Whether they entered Yellowstone Park at this time is entirely conjectural. In the spring of 1812 they were attacked by Crow Indians near the Three Forks, and Detaye was killed.

On June 29, 1812, seven men led by Robert Stuart left Astoria carrying dispatches overland to Astor. The party arrived at St. Louis on April 30, 1813. They were the first organized transcontinental expedition eastbound after the return of Lewis and Clark, and the first to discover South Pass and the great Platte or Central route which was destined to become the main highway of the covered-wagon migrations. This journey again took them through Jackson's Hole.

Stuart had gone out to Astoria by sea, but his fellow travelers had all been members of the Hunt expedition. These were John Day, Benjamin Jones, Francois Leclerc, Andre Valle, Ramsay Crooks, and Robert McClellan. Soon after setting out up the Columbia River John Day became violently deranged because of his sufferings from the previous winter and had to be sent back to Astoria. To the six remaining travelers, however, was eventually added Joseph Miller, who had been with Hoback, Robinson, and Reznor after they left Hunt in October 1811. The Stuart party reached Bear River intending to go due east; but there Crow Indians got on their trail. To elude them Stuart went north to the Snake and thus struck Hunt's route of the preceding year. At Snake or "Mad River" near the present Idaho-Wyoming boundary, Crows stampeded their horses. They built a raft and descended the Snake for over a hundred miles, then crossed over the Snake River Range to Pierre's Hole at the foot of the "Pilot Knobs," where they reached familiar territory.

Here, in order to avoid a chance encounter with a Blackfoot war party, Stuart kept to the foothills, but the cantankerous McClellan, complaining of sore feet, refused to detour and went his own way. He was not to be seen again for thirteen days. Crooks, who had been ailing for some time, fell desperately ill, and despite recourse to castor oil and "an Indian sweat," tied up the expedition in Pierre's Hole for four days. On October 5 they set out again and on the 7th crossed "the summit of Pilot Knob Mountain [Teton Pass]" and reached the east bank of "Mad River." Their stock of venison was by this time depleted. On the 9th they started up the precipitous Hoback Canyon and on the 12th reached Green River drainage, where they found McClellan. Warding off starvation by slaughtering an "old rundown buffalo bull," the travelers journeyed from here to South Pass and down the Platte, wintering in the vicinity of Scotts Bluff.

For a few years after Stuart's party disappeared up Hoback Canyon, the Tetons and Jackson's Hole were left in solitude. Due to the hostility of the Blackfeet, the loss of Astoria in the War of 1812, and the indifference of the Federal Government, American interest in the Western Fur trade suffered a relapse. British interests now took the initiative. In 1816 the Northwest Company, licensed by the Crown to trade in Oregon, put Donald McKenzie in charge of the Snake River division. From Fort Nez Perce at the mouth of the Walla Walla, he set forth in September of 1818 at the head of an expedition "composed of fifty-five men, of all denominations, 195 horses and 300 beaver traps, besides a considerable stock of merchandise." He reported his course to Alexander Ross:

> From this place [the "Skamnaugh" or Boise] we advanced, suffering occasionally from alarms for twenty-five days, and then found ourselves in a rich field of beaver, in the country lying between the great south branch and the Spanish waters [Bear River?]. . . . I left my people at the end of four months. Then taking a circuitous route along the foot of the Rocky Mountains, a country extremely dreary during a winter voyage, I reached the head water of the great south branch regretting every step I made that we had been so long deprived of the riches of such a country. . . .

In a description of the Snake River country, presumably furnished him by McKenzie, Ross continues:

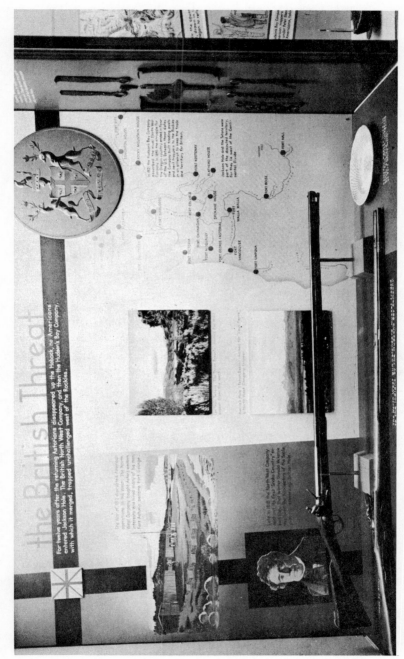

"The British Threat"—Exhibit in Fur Trade Museum, Grand Teton National Park.

The Rocky Mountains skirting this country on the East, dwindle from stupendous heights into sloping ridges, which divide the country into a thousand luxurious vales, watered by streams which abound in fish. The most remarkable heights in any part of the great backbone of America are three elevated insular mountains, or peaks, which are seen at the distance of one hundred and fifty miles: the hunters very aptly designate them the Pilot Knobs they are now generally known as the Three Paps or 'Tetons'; and the source of the Great Snake River is in their neighborhood. . . .

Boiling fountains, having different degrees of temperatures, were very numerous; one or two were so very hot as to boil meat. In other parts, among the rocks, hot and cold springs might alternately be seen within a hundred yards of each other, differing in their temperature.

McKenzie's exact route can only be conjectural, but the context suggests passage through Jackson's Hole into a corner, at least, of Yellowstone Park. It was apparently on this occasion that the "Trois Tetons" and "Pierre's Hole" were given their names by Iroquois or French-Canadians who accompanied McKenzie.

Chittenden reports the discovery in 1880 by Colonel P. W. Norris of a tree near the Upper Falls of the Yellowstone with the inscription "JOR Aug 19 1819." Although of course the initials prove nothing as to identity, Chittenden accepts this as proof of white men in the Park at that time.

Stimulated by McKenzie's success in acquiring peltries, the Northwest Company followed up with other Snake River expeditions. The threat of British domination of Oregon was aggravated when, in 1821, the Northwest Company was absorbed by the powerful Hudson's Bay Company.

Shortly after the consolidation of the British companies, the prospects for a revival of American interest in the mountain fur trade were awakened in the frontier town of St. Louis by the formation of a partnership that would evolve into the Rocky Mountain Fur Company. In 1822 General William H. Ashley and the veteran Major Andrew Henry enlisted the aid of "one hundred young men to ascend the Missouri River to its source" on a trapping expedition. Among those who joined the enterprise, then or subse-

quently, were men destined to make history in the West—
James Bridger, Thomas Fitzpatrick, Jedediah Smith, William
Sublette and David E. Jackson. They were green boys,
hardly fit material for an epic invasion of the unchartered
Rocky Mountains; yet they were destined to become con-
tinental explorers.

Henry took his young men in keelboats up the Missouri
to the mouth of the Yellowstone, where they spent the
winter. In the spring of 1823 he set out for the Blackfoot
country to the west. Again, as in 1810, these Indians proved
to be most inhospitable, scalping four of his recruits and
driving him back to his fort. Meanwhile General Ashley
organized another expedition and proceeded upriver without
incident until he arrived at the villages of the Arikara.
There his plans were upset by a treacherous attack in which
thirteen of his men were killed and many others were
wounded. Colonel Leavenworth hastened to the rescue,
but his campaign against the Indians was something of a
fiasco. Soon afterward Ashley returned to St. Louis, Henry
returned to his post on the Yellowstone, and a third con-
tingent started overland under the command of Jedediah
Smith. In February 1824 this last group made the first
crossing of South Pass from east to west, their discovery of
rich beaver fields in Green River Basin opening a new era
in fur trade history. In June they split into four parties.
Fitzpatrick, heading east for Fort Atkinson to report the
situation to Ashley, rediscovered the Platte route of the
returning Astorians; Sublette, Bridger, and others went
southwest to explore the Bear River country and lay claim
to the discovery of Great Salt Lake; and Smith, with six
unidentified companions, went north. The details of their
course are given in Washington Hood's **Original draft of a
report of a practicable route for wheeled vehicles across the
mountains,** written at Independence, August 12, 1839.

> After striking the Colorado, or Green river, make up the
> stream toward its headwaters, as far as Horse creek, one of
> its tributaries, follow out this last mentioned stream to its
> source by a westerly course, across the main ridge in order
> to attain Jackson's Little Hole, at the headwaters of Jack-
> son's fork [Hoback River]. Follow down Jackson's fork
> to its mouth and decline to the northward along Lewis's

fork [Snake River], passing through Jackson's Big Hole to about twelve miles beyond the Yellowstone pass [sic], crossing on the route a nameless beaver stream. Here the route passes due west over another prong of the ridge [Conant Pass], a fraction worse than the former, followed until it has attained the headwaters of Pierre's Hole, crossing the Big Teton, the battleground of the Blacksmith's fork; ford Pierre's fork eastward of the butte at its mouth and Lewis fork also, thence pass to the mouth of Lewis fork.

Subsequently the Smith party encountered a Hudson's Bay Company brigade under Alexander Ross, giving first notice that Americans would actively contest British claims to Oregon. This expedition to the Jackson's Hole country was also significant as the first in an amazing series which has established Jedediah Smith as perhaps the foremost explorer of Western America.

We have noted the visit of McKenzie's brigade of British-Canadians to the Upper Snake and a region of boiling fountains, in 1818-1819, as reported by Ross. Now, in 1824, Ross himself conducted the second British invasion of Yellowstone Park, while crossing from Okanagon to the headwaters of the Missouri. In the foolscap folios which make up his official report, the entry for April 24 reads: "We crossed beyond the Boiling Fountains. The snow is knee-deep half the people are snow-blind from sun glare." So British traders have supplied the first clear record of Yellowstone thermal wonders to follow the hazy notations along Colter's route on The Clark Map of 1810.

TRADE BEADS
AND
HAWK BELLS

VI. "Jackson's Hole": Era of the Rocky Mountain Fur Company, 1825-1832

Late in 1824 General Ashley, journeying west to reap the winter's harvest of furs, approached the mountains by way of the little-known South Platte route and the Colorado Rockies and explored the lower Green River. In the summer of 1825 on Henry's Fork of the Green (near the Wyoming-Utah line) he inaugurated the annual rendezvous of the mountain trappers, which provided a more flexible system of fur trading than the "fixed fort system" which had hitherto prevailed in the Western fur trade. The beaver catch brought in this first year was of such magnitude that Ashley was assured of a substantial profit. With Smith and a strong guard he took his prize by pack train to the Bighorn, by bullboats to the mouth of the Yellowstone, and by keelboats down the Missouri River to St. Louis.

Jedediah Smith left Flathead House in 1825 with Peter Skene Ogden of the Hudson's Bay Company, but left him in time to rejoin his comrades at the rendezvous. When the reunited Americans exchanged tales of their adventures, it is possible that Smith offered a glowing account of the Jackson's Hole region. Whatever the inspiration, Bridger and Fitzpatrick are reported to have headed there to resume trapping operations, after seeing Smith and Ashley safely down the Bighorn. This may have been the first large-scale trapping venture in which Jackson's Hole was a primary objective.

The rendezvous of 1826 took place near Great Salt Lake. The turnover of furs was immense and, having made his fortune, General Ashley sold his interests to three of his most able employees, Jedediah Smith, David E. Jackson, and William Sublette. Smith left the rendezvous to lead a band southwest across the desert to the Spanish settlements of California, being the first to make this perilous passage. Jackson and Sublette headed for the Snake River country to trade with the Flatheads, taking a large force of trappers.

Daniel T. Potts of Montgomery County, Pennsylvania, one of Sublette's men on this expedition, is now identified as the long-mysterious author of the letter which first appeared in the Philadelphia **Gazette and Daily Advertiser,** September 27, 1827, reprinted in **Niles' Register** of October 6, which contains the earliest known description of any portion of present Yellowstone National Park by an American. The original document came to light in 1947 when Mrs. Kate Nixon and Miss Anne G. Rittenhouse of Washington, D. C., collateral descendants of Potts, made themselves known to officials of the National Park Service. It has been fittingly acquired for posterity by the Yellowstone Library and Museum Association at Mammoth Hot Springs. The cover is addressed to "Mr. Robert T. Potts, High Street, Philadelphia" and stamped "St. Louis, Missouri." Dated July 8, 1827, at the "Sweet Lake" or Bear Lake (Utah) rendezvous, it describes how the Potts party, no members of which are identified, went north after the Salt Lake rendezvous of 1826:

> A few dass sinci our trader arived by whom I received two letters one from Dr. Lukens the other from yourself under date of January 1827 which gives me great congratulation to hear that you are both happy wilst I am unhappy also to hear from my friends shortly after writing to you last year I took my departuri for the Black-foot Country much against my will as I could not maki a party for any other rout. We took a northerly direction about fifty miles where we cross Snake River or the South fork of columbia at the forks of Henrys & Lewis's forks at this place we was dayly harrased by the Black-feet from thence up Henrys or North fork which bears North of East thirty

miles and crossed a large ruged Mountain which sepparates the two forks from thence East up the other fork to its source which heads on the top of the great chain of Rocky Mountains which sepparates the water of the Atlantic from that of the Pacific. At or near this place heads the Luch-kadee or Calliforn Stinking fork Yellow-stone South fork of Massuri and Henrys fork all those head at an angular point that of the Yellow-stone has a large fresh water lake near its head on the verry top of the Mountain which is about one hundrid by fourty miles in diameter and as clear as crystal on the south borders of this lake is a number of hot and boiling springs some of water and others of most beautiful fine clay and resembles that of a mush pot and throws its particles to the immense height of from twenty to thirty feet in height The clay is white and of a pink and water appear fathomless as it appears to be entirely hollow under neath. There is also a number of places where the pure suphor is sent forth in abundance one of our men Visited one of those wilst taking his recreation there at an instan the earth began a tremendious trembling and he with dificulty made his escape when an explosion took place resembling that of thunder. During our stay in that quarter I head it every day.

From here, probably the West Thumb thermal area, "by a circutous rout to the Nourth west" and after some more bloody encounters with the Blackfeet, the trappers moved toward the Bear Lake rendezvous. In 1828 Potts left the hostile mountains and embarked from New Orleans on a cattle ship, which sank with all hands in the Gulf of Mexico.

At the 1827 rendezvous at Bear Lake Jedediah Smith appeared like a ghost out of the Great Salt desert, reporting

Daniel T. Potts at the Bear Lake rendezvous of 1827.

37

that the Spanish Governor of California had expelled him
from that province. He arranged with his partners, Jackson
and Sublette, to meet two years hence "at the head of
Snake River." Then, after a rest of only ten days, he
summoned volunteers and again set his face toward the
Pacific Ocean. In the winter of 1827-28, while Sublette
attended to the business of getting supplies from St. Louis,
Jackson sent fur brigades north from Bear Lake to the
Snake River and its tributaries, where they came in frequent
contact with the Hudson's Bay Company trappers under
Ogden. In 1828 the rendezvous was again Great Salt Lake,
and again the trappers dispersed to hunting grounds on
the Bear, the Snake, and the Green.

In March 1829 William Sublette left St. Louis for the
mountains with a heavily laden pack train and 60 men, including a novice of 19 named Joseph L. Meek, whose life
story, as told to Mrs. F. F. Victor, is a prime source of information. After the general rendezvous, which that year
was held in July on the Popo Agie River northeast of South
Pass, Captain Sublette sent a brigade under his brother,
Milton Sublette, to the Bighorn Basin, then set out with the
main party, including Meek, Bridger, and Fitzpatrick, for
the upper Snake River Valley at the foot of the Tetons, the

Keelboat up the Missouri.

38

Arikara attack on Ashley Party, 1823.

point of reunion with his partners which had been agreed upon two years previously. The episode which followed, one of the treasured traditions of the Western fur trade, is described in Mrs. Victor's **River of the West:**

> Sublette led his company up the valley of the Wind River, across the mountains, and on to the very headwaters of the Lewis or Snake River. Here he fell in with Jackson, in the valley of Lewis Lake, called Jackson's Hole, and remained on the borders of this lake for some time, waiting for Smith, whose non-appearance began to create a good deal of uneasiness. At length runners were dispatched in all directions looking for the lost Booshway.

> The detachment to which Meek was assigned had the pleasure and honor of discovering the hiding place of the missing partner, which was in Pierre's Hole, a mountain valley about thirty miles long and of half that width, which subsequently was much frequented by the camps of the various fur companies.

This is the core of the tradition. From this it has generally been inferred that it was on this occasion that the lake and the valley were named in honor of David E. Jackson, and that this was Captain Sublette's idea. David E. Jackson, sometimes referred to as "Davey," is the mystery man of the Smith-Jackson-Sublette trio. How old he was, what he looked like, where he came from prior to 1823 is not known. He was one of the "enterprising young men"

39

who responded to Ashley's call in that year. That his "rating" with trappers was high and that he was one of the acknowledged leaders of the Rocky Mountain fur trade is clear from the fact of the partnership formed in 1826. He was not illiterate, for his signature appears on documents, but like most of his associates he kept no diary, so that our knowledge of his exact wanderings is indistinct. It is part of the tradition that he spent the winter of 1828-29 in the vicinity of Jackson's Hole, and his known interest in the region prompts us to believe that he had spent several previous years there as well. He might well have been one of the six men who accompanied Smith on his "discovery" of Jackson Hole in 1824. He left the mountains in 1830, went to Santa Fe and then on to California on a trading venture in 1831, and apparently returned to St. Louis in 1832, where he disappears, so to speak, under a cloud. One rumor has it that he "ran off with property belonging to the firm of Jackson, Waldo and Young," another that "he dissipated his large and hard-earned fortune in a few years."

After the reunion in Pierre's Hole, according to Meek, the entire company moved up Henry's Fork of the Snake, and across the Divide to the valleys of the Madison and Gallatin. Crossing the Gallatin Range in early winter, the trappers reached the vicinity of Cinnabar Mountain, three miles below Yellowstone Park's present North Entrance. Here two men were killed and the party was scattered by the Blackfeet. Meek alleges that he wandered into the future Park, where he ascended a high peak. Crossing Yellowstone River, he ran into an incredible region smoking "like Pittsburgh on a winter morning" with the vapor from boiling springs, haunted by the sound of whistling steam vents, dotted with cone-shaped mounds surmounted by craters from which issued "blue flames and molten brimstone," and devoid of living creatures. From here, apparently the seldom visited Mirror Plateau, Meek crossed the Absaroka Range to the winter camp on Powder River.

About the first of April 1830, according to Meek, "Jackson, or 'Davey,' as he was called by his men, with about half the company, left for the Snake country." At the Wind River rendezvous in July, "Jackson arrived from the Snake country with plenty of beaver. . . ."

At Wind River, on August 4, 1830, Smith, Jackson, and Sublette, having earned a deserved fortune from their labors, decided to retire from the mountain trade, and sold their interest to a group of their employees who had already distinguished themselves in the service—James Bridger, Thomas Fitzpatrick, Milton Sublette, Henry Fraeb, and Baptiste Gervais. The main trapper band, numbering over two hundred and including Meek, followed Bridger and Fitzpatrick northward to the Three Forks of the Missouri, thence south to Ogden's Hole, a small valley in the Bear River Mountains. In the fall of 1830, John Work, heading the annual Snake River expedition of the Hudson's Bay Company, got wind of the American invasion of his domain. Among other rumors was one that Fontenelle and his men "have been hunting on the Upper Snake. They were set upon by the Blackfeet on the Yellowstone River and 18 men killed."

In the spring of 1831, after wintering again at Powder River, Meek reports on the spring hunt: "Having once more visited the Yellowstone, they turned to the south again, crossing the mountains into Pierre's Hole, on to Snake river; thence to Salt river; thence to Bear river; and thence to Green river to rendezvous." Confirmation of this comes from Joseph Meek's brother Stephen, who says that this year he trapped on the Yellowstone, Wind, and Musselshell Rivers, "going through Jackson's Hole to the rendezvous on Popyoisa River."

From the Powder River encampment Fitzpatrick headed for St. Louis to round up a supply caravan. Running into his old companions Smith, Jackson, and Sublette en route to Santa Fe, he was persuaded to join them, being promised an outfit when they arrived. Thus he shared the delays and perils of that expedition in which Jedediah Smith was slain by a Comanche spear, and when he left Santa Fe, he

41

was far behind schedule. Picking up young Kit Carson and other volunteers at Taos, he followed the east slope of the Rockies into eastern Wyoming country, sometime during September reaching the North Platte River at Laramie's Fork. Here he met Fraeb, who had been sent to look for him while the others waited impatiently with parched tongues at Green River. Fitzpatrick returned to St. Louis for supplies, while Fraeb led the recruits westward, traveling via Green River and Jackson's Hole to "winter quarters on the head of Salmon River." Thus there was no real summer rendezvous in 1831.

At this time the shadow of the American Fur Company, the great monopoly of the Upper Missouri region, fell across the Rocky Mountains. In February 1830 the newly organized "Western Department" of this company, determined to capture the lucrative mountain trade, sent out an expedition from St. Louis under Andrew Drips, Lucien Fontenelle and one Robidoux. Our chief source of information about this company during the early 1830's is the journal of Warren A. Ferris. From an encampment near the Big Hole country of Montana, Ferris writes: "On the 8th [of October, 1831] two of our men accompanied by three or four Indians departed for the Trois Tetons, to meet Mr. Dripps who was expected this fall from the Council Bluffs, with an equipment of men, horses, and merchandise."

From spring camping grounds on the Bear and Snake River tributaries, the brigades of the rival companies converged on Pierre's Hole, where the Rocky Mountain Fur Company partners had scheduled their rendezvous for 1832. Although they welcomed peaceful Indians and "free" trappers, they expressly did not invite their competitors of the American Fur Company who, nevertheless decided to attend. Rumors of the impending conclave of the "mountain men" also reached the scattered bands of independent trappers, among whom was George Nidever. In the spring Nidever's band trapped up the Green River until May, intending to continue on to "the head waters of the Columbia," but turned back when they learned that "the place we intended going was already being trapped by other companies." (This strongly suggests that somebody, probably Rocky Mountain men, were trapping in Jackson's Hole prior to the rendezvous.) Returning to the Platte River, they met "O'Felon" and Moses "Black" Harris, two other independent traders, with whom they proceeded by way of Teton Pass to the rendezvous, where they arrived on July 4.

The experienced William Sublette, one-time partner, had contracted with the Rocky Mountain Fur Company to supply trade goods, and to take out the beaver hides. With Robert Campbell he set out for St. Louis in May 1832 with over 100 men. At Independence he picked up a band of eighteen green New Englanders under Nathaniel J. Wyeth, an ambitious young man who had hopes of succeeding, where John Jacob Astor had failed, in establishing a fur-trading empire in Oregon. At Laramie's Fork he recruited some twenty trappers under Alfred K. Stephens, and other trappers were picked up farther on. Not the least remarkable feature of this expedition was that at least five of its members kept notes—William Sublette, the methodical Nathaniel Wyeth, his brother John B. Wyeth, another of his followers named John Ball, and Zenas Leonard, one of the "free" trappers with Stephens.

Sublette's acount is contained in a letter to General Ashley, dated Lexington, Missouri, September 21, 1832. He indicates that he arrived at the head of the "Colorado of the West" (Green River) on July 2, being attacked that night by Blackfoot Indians; arrived "on the waters of the Columbia" July 4 "and at the rendezvous of the Rocky Mountain Hunters, on the Columbia river, west of the Three Teton Mountains," on July 8. Nathaniel Wyeth's diary agrees substantially with Sublette on chronology, but is much more illuminating. He clearly depicts the dangerous descent of the Hoback, the fording of "Lewis River" on July 6, and the climb up Teton Pass, "a gap of the mountains due south of the Trois Tetons." The disillusioned brother, John Wyeth, gives us a dramatic picture:

43

On the 4th [6th?] of July, 1832, we arrived at Lewis's fork [Snake River], one of the largest rivers in these rocky mountains. It took us all day to cross it. It is half a mile wide, deep and rapid. The way we managed was this: one man unloaded his horse, and swam across with him, leading two loaded ones, and unloading the two, brought them back, for two more, and as Sublet's company and our own made over a hundred and fifty, we were all day in passing the river. In returning, my mule, by treading on a round stone, stumbled and threw me off, and the current was so strong, that a bush which I caught hold of only saved me from drowning.

"Broken Hand" Fitzpatrick became "White Hair" Fitzpatrick as a result of events which befell him in 1832. Zenas Leonard states that in June 1832 while he was encamped at Laramie's Fork:

Mr. Fitzpatrick and a company of 115 men came to our camp. He was on his way [from St. Louis] to join his company on the west side of the mountains, on the Columbia River, and to supply them with merchandise, ammunition, horses, etc. . . .

Having made this arrangement with Mr. F., our camp [on the Laramie] was all confusion at an early hour this morning, preparing to depart for the Columbia river. Mr. F. took one of the fleetest and most hardy horses in his train, and set out in advance of the main body, in order to discover the disposition of the various Indian tribes through whose dominions we were to travel, and to meet us at a designated point on the head of the Columbia river.

While en route to Pierre's Hole, probably in the valley of Green River, Fitzpatrick was ambushed by or stumbled upon the hostile Gros Ventres, probably the same who later raided Sublette's camp. By sacrificing his horse and secreting himself in a hole in the rocks, he managed to elude these savages, but nearly starved while wandering through the wilderness. Fitzpatrick's whereabouts during his ordeal are not recorded, and in most accounts he merely turns up (on July 8, according to Ferris) in Pierre's Hole in a pitiful state. Meek relates that "he made his appearance in camp in company with two Iroquois half-breeds, belonging to the camp, who had been out on a hunt," which is also the way that Irving got it from Bonneville. George Nidever claims to have been one of these hunters, and, if his story is straight, Fitzpatrick was found in Jackson's Hole: "A week or so after the arrival of the company a trapper by the name of Poe and I went out for a short hunt, and met Fitzpatrick crossing the Lewis Fork. . . . We piloted him back to camp."

By the 17th of July the whiskey kegs were all empty, and the wild celebration which invariably climaxed every rendezvous of the fur traders perforce came to an end in Pierre's Hole. On this day the combined companies of Nathaniel Wyeth and Milton Sublette set out for the lower Snake River. On the morning of the 18th they described a column of Gros Ventre tribesmen descending a hillside, "fantastically painted and arrayed, with scarlet blankets fluttering in the wind." The ensuing conflict was a victory for the trappers. Some of the Indians escaped from their improvised fort into Jackson's Hole, leaving perhaps twenty-six of their number dead, while their trail of blood suggested other heavy casualties. This battle upset the general time-table and delayed the various departures from the rendez-vous. On the 24th of July, Wyeth and Milton Sublette re-sumed their journey which had before been so rudely in-terrupted, Wyeth eventually continuing on to visit the Brit-ish establishments on the Pacific Coast. Captain Sublette was compelled to linger because of his injuries, and, on the 25th, seven who planned to accompany him to St. Louis became impatient and started out by themselves. These were Joseph More of Boston, one of Wyeth's deserters, a Mr. Foy of Mississippi, Alfred K. Stephens, "two grandsons of the celebrated Daniel Boone," and two others unidentified. In Jackson's Hole, apparently near the mouth of the Hoback, they were ambushed by a band of Gros Ventres. More and Foy were killed instantly, while Stephens died from his wounds after he and the four survivors retreated with tid-ing of disaster to Sublette's camp.

On July 30 Bridger and Fitzpatrick led the Rocky Mountain Fur Company brigades northward from Pierre's Hole toward the headwaters of the Missouri, while William Sublette found himself sufficiently recovered to assist Campbell in organizing the homeward-bound caravan, com-posed of sixty men and a beaver-laden packtrain. Accord-ing to Irving, "they chose a different route through the mountains, out of the way, as they hoped, of the lurking bands of Blackfeet. They succeeded in making the frontier in safety." It seems evident that the Sublette caravan turned north after crossing the Snake and then ascended the Gros Ventre River and crossed over to Wind River by way of Union Pass. While the Sublette caravan was leaving the valley, they were shadowed by a "large body of the Blackfoot tribe," doubtless the murderers of More and Foy, who showed a healthy respect for the heavily armed trappers. Thus it would seem that, while he did not entirely elude the Blackfeet, Sublette managed to bluff his way past them and avoid what might well have become the "Battle of Jackson's Hole."

At the Pierre's Hole rendezvous, Drips and Vanderburgh, the American Fur Company partisans, were frustrated in their competitive effort by the fact that their supply train under Fontenelle had failed to arrive. It was now too late to bid for the furs taken out by Sublette, but they might follow Bridger and Fitzpatrick with profit if they only had trade goods. Accordingly, they resolved to hasten to Green River to see if they could find the belated caravan. The clerk, Warren A. Ferris, gives a detailed account of the passage through "Jackson's Big Hole," in early August:

> In the evening we halted on a spring, four miles east of Lewis River, after marching twenty-two miles. On the 5th we passed six or eight miles southeast, and halted on the margin of the stream [Hoback], flowing from that direction. During our march, some of the hunters saw the bones of two men, supposed to be those killed from a party of seven, in the latter part of July. . . .

After losing one horse in precipitous Hoback Canyon, the party reached Jackson's Little Hole, where they killed several buffalo, and successfully by-passed a large village of Indians. They crossed over to Green River, and on the 8th fell in with Fontenelle, "who had passed from St. Louis to the mouth of the Yellowstone in a steamboat, and thence with pack horses to this place." Ferris accompanied Vanderburgh and Drips on the return trip in pursuit of Bridger. He writes:

On the 14th we passed through the Narrows, between Jackson's Holes; and avoided some of the difficulties we met on our previous passage, by crossing the river, several times. In the evening we halted for the night near the remains of two men, who were killed in July last. These we collected, and deposited in a small stream, that discharged itself into a fork of the Lewis river; that flows from Jackson's Little Hole.

Captain Benjamin L. E. Bonneville, a Frenchman of distinguished antecedents, applied in 1831 for a leave of absence from the U.S. Army for the joint purpose of exploration and trade. With funds provided by hopeful New York capitalists he organized an impressive company, including 110 men and twenty ox-drawn wagons, and on May 1, 1832, he set out from Fort Osage. Bonneville's wagon train was the second to ascend the traditional overland route along the Platte and the Sweetwater, and the first to cross South Pass. In the Green River Valley on July 26 the Captain was overtaken by Fontenelle's company. On the west side of the Green, five miles above Horse Creek, he started the erection of Fort Bonneville, while his rival encamped farther upstream, for his jaded horses and mules would budge no further. After Fontenelle's departure, above noted, the Captain decided upon the advice of "free trappers," to head for Salmon River for the winter. Leaving his cumbersome wagons at the fort, he cached most of his

Rendezvous scene.

47

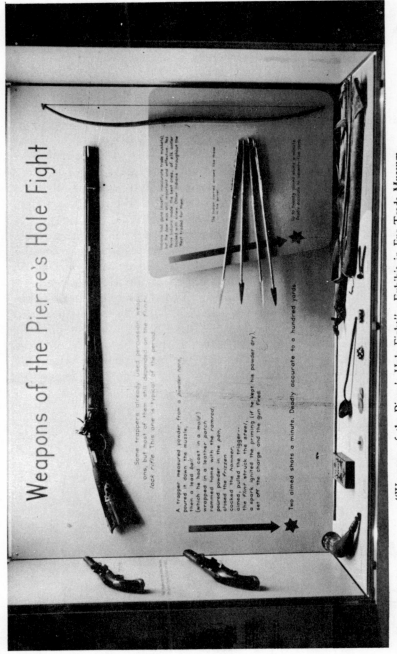

"Weapons of the Pierre's Hole Fight"—Exhibit in Fur Trade Museum, Grand Teton National Park.

baggage and then packed the rest on mules and horses. The expedition set forth on August 22, reaching Teton Pass on September 3. Instead of taking the standard route via the Hoback, where hostile Indians waited in ambush, Captain Bonneville elected to take a long circuitous route to the headwaters of Green River, entering Jackson's Hole via the Gros Ventre River.

Following the rendezvous in Pierre's Hole, the Rocky Mountain men conducted their fall hunt in the dangerous Blackfoot country around the Three Forks of the Missouri. In attempting to follow them, Vanderburgh of the American Fur Company was slain by the Blackfeet. During the winter of 1832-33 the various rival bands holed up along tributaries of the Snake and Salmon rivers; and at the first melting of the snow they resumed their feverish scramble for the prime hunting grounds.

Most of the other trapping bands remained west of the Continental Divide to make their spring hunt, and approached the Green River rendezvous through Jackson's Hole. The first to stir in this direction was the American Fur Company partisan Drips, who led the bulk of his forces, probably about sixty men, up Snake River, hunting and trapping as they went. At the junction of Salt River, they were compelled to leave the Snake to make the toilsome detour over the Snake River Range and Teton Pass, which they reached on May 31. Ferris vividly describes their journey through the "immense banks of snow on the mountain," the fording of "Lewis River," and the ascent of "Gros Vent's Fork" to the head of Green River. He notes, "We found a large herd of buffalo in the valley, and killed several; also a large bear, which paid with his life the temerity of awaiting our approach."

Wyeth's enterprise on the Columbia River was balked by the shipwreck of the vessel which was to supply him, and, after a fruitless winter at Fort Vancouver, he set out eastward with Francis Ermatinger of the Hudson's Bay Company. Below the forks of the Snake they came up with

Captain Bonneville. The Wyeth journal tells the story of their Jackson's Hole passage via Teton Pass and the Hoback. He found "horse flies on the mountains . . . buffalo in the bottom also mosquitoes." Evidence of the recent trail of the "men of Dripps and Fontenelle" was observed, also the place where More and Foy were killed the year before. Of this passage Irving reports,

> No accident of a disastrous kind occurred, excepting the loss of a horse, which, in passing along the giddy edge of a precipice, called the Cornice, a dangerous pass between Jackson's and Pierre's Hole, fell over the brink, and was dashed to pieces.

On the 13th of July [1833], Captain Bonneville arrived at Green River. . . .

Fort Bonneville site, on Horse Creek near its junction with Green River.
Photo by Author

Section of "Map of the Rocky Mountains" by Washington Hood, Corps of Topographical Engineers. 1839. Data by William Sublette and others. Records of the War Department, National Archives.

51

Trapper type—American.

BULLET MOLD

VII. "The Fire Hole": Era of the American Fur Company, 1833-1840

By 1832 only fragments of the Yellowstone Park area had apparently been explored, notably the Lake region. According to Warren A. Ferris, one of the great geyser basins was visited in the spring hunt of 1833 by a party of forty men under a Spaniard named Alvaris (or Alvarez). They reached the area by going up Henry's Fork, later returning to Green River for the rendezvous. This is the first concrete evidence of white men in the Firehole Basin. The discoverer may have been Manuel Alvarez, United States consul at Santa Fe from 1839 to 1846, who figures prominently in Josiah Gregg's journal.

The rendezvous of 1833 was held at Bonneville's fort on Horse Creek, tributary of Green River, near Daniel, Wyoming. The St. Louis supply caravan of the Rocky Mountain Fur Company, led by Robert Campbell, included young Charles Larpenteur, who wrote in his journal of a side trip through Jackson's Hole:

> The day after we reached the rendezvous Mr. Campbell,, with ten men, started to raise a beaver cache at a place called by the French Trou a Pierre, which means Peter's Hole. As I was sick Mr. Campbell left me in camp, and placed Mr. Fitzpatrick in charge during his absence, telling the latter to take good care of me . . . after seven or eight days Mr. Campbell returned with ten packs of beaver.

An epidemic of hydrophobia brought on by "mad wolves" seems to have contributed to the early break-up of the 1833 meeting. Campbell, Wyeth, and the partners of the Rocky Mountain Fur Company with fifty-five packs of beaver and a strong guard circled down through South Pass and up to the junction of the Shoshone and the Bighorn rivers, where they embarked on bullboats for the mouth of the Yellowstone. Here Wyeth was entertained at the palatial Fort Union by the famous Kenneth McKenzie, and observed a powder flask which had belonged to the unfortunate More, and which had found its way here from Jackson's Hole by the devious channels of the fur trade.

While Bonneville outfitted an expedition under Joseph R. Walker to explore California (and discover Yosemite Valley), the American Fur Company brigades headed for the Snake River country. On July 20 Warren A. Ferris and Robert Newell departed at the head of an outfit destined for the Flathead trade. The little party consisted of six "engages" with pack horses, and five armed Indians, amounting in all to thirteen armed men. Their route was the usual one via Hoback Canyon and Teton Pass. The ecstatic description of Jackson's Hole from the summit of the pass, given by Ferris on this occasion, is one which can be appreciated by the modern tourist:

> . . . Gazing down in the direction of Jackson's Hole, from our elevated position, one of the most beautiful scenes imaginable, was presented to our view. It seemed quite filled with large bright clouds, resembling immense banks of snow, piled on each other in massy numbers, of the purest white; wreathing their ample folds in various forms and devious convolutions, and mingling in one vast embrace their shadowy substance.—Sublime creations! emblems apt of the first glittering imaginings of human life! . . .

> Turning with reluctance to things of a more terrestrial nature we pursued our way down to Pierre's Hole, where we fortunately discovered and killed a solitary bull. . . .

The rendezvous of 1834 was scheduled for June on Ham's Fork of the Green near present Granger, Wyoming; and here converged all the scattered trapper bands, with the exception of those in the pay of Bonneville, who had his own private rendezvous on Bear River. Drips hunted up the Snake River to Jackson's Hole, and apparently crossed into the valley of the Green from there. Behind him came Ferris. On his southward journey from Montana country, Ferris decided to make a side trip from Henry's Fork to investigate strange rumors concerning the upper Madison, a trip which resulted in the second known published description of the Yellowstone Park wonders.

Ferris, a native of New York who later resided in Texas, made his first western journey with the American Fur Company in 1830. Hardly a typical mountain man, he kept a journal of his travels entitled "Life in the Rocky Mountains," which appeared serially in 1842 and 1843 in the **Western Literary Messenger,** an obscure weekly published in Buffalo, New York. The piece containing an account of his visit to the geyser region in 1834 appeared on July 13, 1842, attracted no special attention at the time except that of the editors of the Nauvoo, Illinois, **Wasp,** who ran it without credit in their edition of August 13, 1842. Olin D. Wheeler discovered it and republished it in 1901. Its historical importance as the first adequate description of the geysers by an eyewitness (and the second published description of any portion of Yellowstone Park) was appreciated by Chittenden, but his identity and the magnificent scope of

Fort Hall.

his journal was not fully understood until its republication with extensive editorial notes by Dr. Paul C. Phillips in 1940. It was in May 1834, while his brigade was traveling through Idaho country en route to the rendezvous on Ham's Fork of the Green, that Ferris and two Indian companions made a hurried side trip, going almost due east forty miles. His object was to verify the rumors concerning "remarkable boiling spring on the sources of the Madison" which he had heard at the rendezvous of 1833. He soon realized that "the half was not told me." A fragment of his vivid description follows:

> From the surface of a rocky plain or table, burst forth columns of water, of various dimensions, projected high in the air, accompanied by loud explosions, and sulphurous vapors, which were highly disagreeable to the smell. The rock from which these springs burst forth, was calcareous, and probably extends some distance from them, beneath the soil. The largest of these wonderful fountains, projects a column of boiling water several feet in diameter, to the height of more than one hundred and fifty feet—in my opinion; but the party of Alvarez, who discovered it, persist in declaring that it could not be less than four times that distance in height—accompanied with a tremendous noise. These explosions and discharges occur at intervals of about two hours.

Baling beaver hides inside stockade.

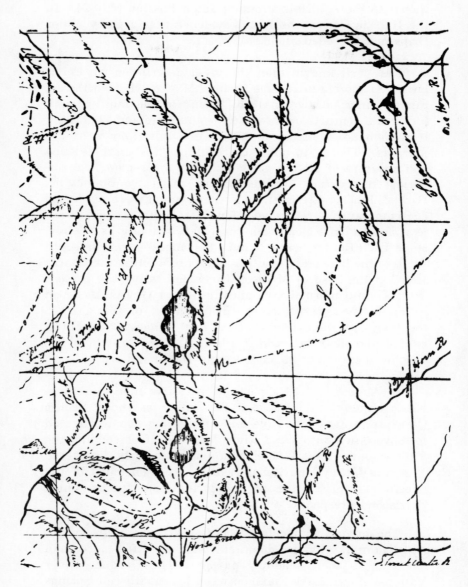

Section of "Map of the Northwest Fur Country," 1836, by Warren A. Ferris. From *Life in the Rocky Mountains*, Old West Publishing Company, Denver, 1940.

After this adventure, he returned to Henry's Fork and thence to Pierre's Hole, crossing Teton Pass on May 24. In the Hoback Canyon he found evidence that a party under Drips had preceded him.

Less well known than the vivid description by Ferris but even more remarkable is his "Map of the Northwest Fur Country," drawn in 1836. Lying in the family trunk for over a century, unknown to geographers and historians, it was made available in 1940 for publication with the journals. This is, to quote Dr. Phillips, "the most detailed and accurate of all the early maps of the region," far superior in accuracy to the famous maps by Bonneville, Parker, John C. Fremont, and others which were published contemporaneously. In addition to mountain chains, valleys, and trails, it locates such fascinating details as "Yellow stone L.," "Boiling water," and "Volcanoes" near the south shore of the lake and "spouting fountains" within the "Burnt Hole" at the head of Madison River, indicating the present West Thumb thermal area and the Upper Geyser Basin on Firehole River, respectively. The context of the journal, together with the evidence of the map, suggests that Ferris beheld and described Old Faithful, the geyser which has become the symbol of Yellowstone National Park.

In August of 1834 a party of fifty-five men in Bonneville's employ led by Joseph H. Walker ascended Pacific Creek from Jackson's Hole and after some debate "agreed to move down onto Wind River," instead of descending the Yellowstone. Thus Walker, who had previously discovered Yosemite Valley, and Zenas Leonard, the journalist of the expedition, missed the big exploring opportunity which Ferris had grasped.

The quaint nomenclature bestowed on certain locales and landmarks by the mountain trappers offer more than one clue to their shadowy passage. The Gardner River Valley at Swan Lake Flats, between Mammoth Hot Springs and Obsidian Cliff, seems to be the most likely locale of the beaver-rich "Gardner's Hole" frequented by the mountain men, probably named for Johnson Gardner, a freelance trapper who must have frequented those parts at least as early as 1834, possibly as early as 1830 as Chittenden suggests. His name appears in the Fort Union account books of 1832, which include an agreement to purchase his stock of beaver skins then cached on Yellowstone River. In 1834 he fell in with Prince Maximilian of Wied on the Lower Missouri, revealing to that distinguished traveler that "he was on his return from hunting beavers on the Upper Yelowstone."

Three significant events occurred in connection with the rendezvous of 1834. (1) En route from St. Louis, Sublette and Campbell began the building of Fort Laramie (originally Fort William) on the North Platte. (2) Nathaniel Wyeth, embarking on a second venture, brought in trade goods which were not accepted, and so resorted to the establishment of Fort Hall near the junction of the Snake and Portneuf. The advent of these two fixed trading posts prophesied an end to the traditional rendezvous system. Also (3), at the rendezvous the partnership of the Rocky Mountain Fur Company was dissolved, Fraeb and Gervais selling out their interests. The remaining partners—Fitzpatrick, Bridger, and Milton Sublette—formed a new firm, but they made an agreement with Fontenelle which gave the American Fur Company a virtual monopoly of the Rocky Mountain fur trade.

Among those whom Nathaniel Wyeth had left at Fort Hall in 1834 was a young man named Osborne Russell, whose subsequent career as a trapper was hardly typical, for among his trapping accessories were copies of Shakespeare and the Bible! Although later a prominent pioneer of Oregon and California, his claim to fame rests on his **Journal of a Trapper,** which "as a precise and intimate firsthand account of the daily life of the trapper explorer . . . has no equal," except that of Warren A. Ferris, who left the mountain scene just as Russell arrived. On the 15th of June 1835 a party of fourteen trappers and ten camp keepers was made up. Writes Russell:

> Here we again fell on to Lewis' Fork, which runs in a southerly direction through a valley about eighty miles long, there turning to the mountains through a narrow cut

59

in the mountain to the mouth of Salt River, about thirty miles. This valley was called 'Jackson Hole.' It is generally from five to fifteen miles wide. The southern part where the river enters the mountains is hilly and uneven, but the northern portion is wide, smooth and comparatively even, the whole being covered with wild sage and surrounded by high and rugged mountains upon whose summit the snow remains during the hottest months in summer. The alluvial bottoms along the river and streams intersecting it through the valley produced a luxuriant growth of vegetation, among which wild flax and a species of onion were abundant. The great altitude of this place, however, connected with the cold descending from the mountains at night, I think would be a serious obstruction to the growth of most kinds of cultivated grains. This valley, like all other parts of the country, abounded with game.

After a nearly disastrous attempt to cross "Lewis Fork" by bullboat and raft, the party discovered a ford, and then ascended Gros Ventre Fork. The party became lost in the mountains for several weeks, missing out on the Green River rendezvous. After extricating themselves from the craggy wilderness of the Absarokas, the party reached the Lamar River or East Fork of the Yellowstone, where they encountered some woebegone Sheepeater Indians, and lost a hunter. They apparently forded the Yellowstone at the lower end of the Grand Canyon near the mouth of Antelope Creek, at a point just above the spectacular Tower Falls and the Basaltic Cliffs where the river "rushes down a chasm with a dreadful roar echoing among the mountains." From "Gardner's Hole" the party then crossed the mountains to Gallatin and Madison forks, where they fell in with a trapping brigade under Bridger. Just below the Madison Canyon the combined forces were attacked by eighty Blackfeet and narrowly escaped massacre.

The supply caravan under Fitzpatrick arrived at the Green River rendezvous on August 12, 1835. Accompanying him were two famous missionaries—Marcus Whitman, who distinguished himself among the trappers by extracting an Indian arrow from the back of Captain Bridger, and Reverend Samuel Parker, who alienated them by his overzealous moralizing. However, Parker made quite a hit with the assembled Flatheads and was so enthusiastic over their eagerness for Christian knowledge that it was decided that he would accompany them to their homes, while Whitman would return to the states to recruit help for a permanent mission in Oregon. Parker tells of his journey westward:

August 21st, commenced our journey in company with Capt. Bridger, who goes with about fifty men, six or eight days' journey on our route. Instead of going down on the southwest side of Lewis' river, we concluded to take our course northerly for the Trois Tetons, which are three very high mountains, covered with perpetual snow, separated from the main chain of the Rocky Mountains, and are seen at a very great distance; and from thence to Salmon river. . . .

On the 22d . . . we . . . arrived at what is called Jackson's Hole [Jackson's Little Hole]. . . .

Sabbath, 23d. Had an opportunity for rest and devotional exercises. In the afternoon we had public worship with those of the company who understood English. The men conducted with great propriety, and listened with attention. . . .

Arose very early on the 24th, and commenced our way through the narrow defile, frequently crossing and recrossing a large stream of water [Hoback] which flows into the Snake river. . . .

. . . on the 25th, [we] encamped in a large pleasant valley, commonly called Jackson's large hole. It is fertile and well watered with a branch of Lewis' river coming from the southeast [Hoback], and another of some magnitude coming from the northeast [Snake River itself], which is the outlet of Jackson's lake, a body of water situated just south of the Trois Tetons. . . .

We continued in this encampment three days, to give our animals an opportunity to recruit, and for Captain Bridger to fit and send out several of his men into the mountains to hunt and trap. . . .

On the 28th, we pursued our journey and passed over a mountain [Teton Pass] so high, that banks of snow were but a short distance from our trail. When we had ascended two-thirds of the way, a number of buffalo, which were pursued by our Indians, came rushing down the side of the mountain through the midst of our company. . . .

In [Pierre's Hole] . . . I parted with Captain Bridger and his party, who went northeast into the mountains to their hunting ground, which the Blackfeet claim, and for which they will contend.

According to the impious Joseph L. Meek, the sermon on Sunday the 23rd in Jackson's Little Hole (the site of which has been memorialized by the State of Wyoming as that of "the first Protestant sermon in the Rocky Mountains") was not such a great success as Parker makes out, for, "in the midst of the discourse, a band of buffalo appeared in the valley, when the congregation broke up, without staying for a benediction," and every man excitedly joined in the hunt.

Another who accompanied this expedition was Kit Carson. Parker gave Carson his initial shove into immortality by relating the story of his victory at the rendezvous over a "great bully" named Shunar:

Marcus Whitman removing arrow from Jim Bridger.

Trappers at Old Faithful.

. . . I will relate an occurrence which took place near evening, as a specimen of mountain life. A hunter, who goes technically by the name of the great bully of the mountains, mounted his horse with a loaded rifle, and challenged any Frenchman, American, Spaniard, or Dutchman, to fight him in single combat. Kit Carson, an American, told him if he wished to die, he would accept the challenge. Shunar defied him. C. mounted his horse, and with a loaded pistol, rushed into close contact, and both almost at the same instant fired. C's ball entered S's hand, came out at the wrist, and passed through the arm above the elbow. Shunar's ball passed over the head of Carson; and while he went for another pistol, Shunar begged that his life might be spared. Such scenes, sometimes from passion, and sometimes for amusement, make the pastime of their wild and wandering life.

Another rendezvous was held for the summer of 1836, again on Horse Creek tributary of Green River. Fitzpatrick and Fontenelle arrived with the supply caravan on July 3. with them were the missionaries Marcus Whitman and H. H. Spalding, accompanied by their wives, the first white women ever to attend a rendezvous of the mountain men and doubtless the first to come within 100 miles of the future Grand Teton and Yellowstone Parks. At this meeting Major Joshua Pilcher, as agent for the American Fur Company, formally and legally took over the interests of Bridger, Fitzpatrick, and Fontenelle, thus consolidating the monopoly. The missionaries, accompanied by Hudson's Bay Company agents, followed the Bear River route westward. The fur trappers were left in the mountains with Drips, Fontenelle, and Bridger. Says Osborne Russell

Mr. Bridger's party, as usual, was destined for the Blackfoot country. It contained most of the American trappers and amounted to sixty men. I started with a party of fifteen trappers and two camp keepers, ordered by Mr. Bridger to proceed to the Yellowstone Lake and there await his arrival with the rest of the party.

Russell entered Jackson's Hole by way of the upper Green and Gros Ventre rivers, followed the Snake River north to Jackson Lake, and on August 7 started up Buffalo Fork, to reach Two Ocean Pass. On August 13, he camped at the inlet of Yellowstone Lake, and on the 16th "Mr. Bridger came up with the remainder of the party." They followed along the eastern shore of the lake to its outlet at present

Fishing Bridge, and camped again "in a beautiful plain which extended along the northern extremity of the lake." Russell describes the lake as "about 100 miles in circumference . . . lying in an oblong form south to north, or rather in the shape of a crescent." His further description of the boiling springs, hot steam vents, and the hollow limestone crustation "of dazzling whiteness," apparently in Hayden Valley, ranks him with Potts and Ferris as a pioneer journalist of the Park phenomena.

In 1837 Thomas Fitzpatrick again led the supply train across the plains, picking up Fontenelle at Fort Laramie,

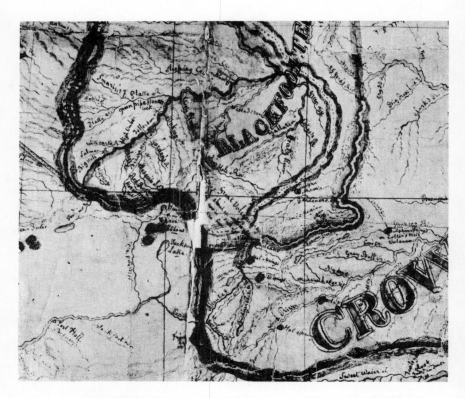

Section of Father DeSmet "map of the Indian country" of 1851, reflecting data given by Jim Bridger. From the Cartographic Section, National Archives.

and arriving at the rendezvous on July 18. After the business of that year was transacted, Drips returned east with Fitzpatrick's caravan, and Fontenelle and Bridger made up a strong company of 110 men to invade the hostile Blackfoot country. Osborne Russell and five others started off separately "to hunt the headwaters of the Yellowstone, Missouri and Bighorn Rivers." Going due north up Green River, they were attacked by "sixty or seventy" Blackfeet, but managed to escape to the rendezvous. Here they wisely decided to throw in with Fontenelle's party, as Russell explains, "intending to keep in their company five or six days and then branch off to our first intended route." After descending the Hoback, Russell and three others left the main party at the ford of "Lewis Fork" in "Jackson's Big Hole" and took the same route to Yellowstone Lake used the preceding year, then went northeast over the mountains to gain the "Stinking Water."

In ths spring of 1838 the company moved westward from Powder River, trapping the Bighorn and other tributaries of the Yellowstone. Russell and Meek report another fight with the Blackfeet on the Madison, followed by a gathering of the brigade on the north fork of the Yellowstone, near the lake. Afterward, Meek reports:

> Bridger's brigade of trappers met with no other serious interruptions on their summer's march. They proceeded to Henry's Lake, and crossing the Rocky Mountains, traveled through the Pine Woods, always a favorite region, to Lewis' Lake on Lewis' Fork of the Snake River [Jackson Lake]; and finally up the Grovant Fork, recrossing the mountains to Wind River, where the rendezvous was appointed.

Osborne Russell describes this rendezvous of 1838:

> . . . [July] 4th—We encamped at the Oil Spring on Popo-azia, and the next day we arrived at the camp. There we found Mr. Dripps from St. Louis, with twenty horse carts loaded with supplies, and again met Captain Stewart, likewise several missionaries with their families on their way to the Columbia River. On the 8th Mr. F. Ermatinger arrived with a small party from the Columbia, accompanied by the Rev. John Lee, who was on his way to the United States. On the 20th of July the meeting broke up and the parties again dispersed for the fall hunt.

66

The Captain Stewart referred to by Russell was an English veteran of Waterloo, Sir William Drummond Stewart, ostensibly a wealthy sportsman, who became a perennial visitor to the annual conclaves of the "mountain men," beginning in 1833. He probably entered Jackson's Hole on more than one occasion, in company with the trapper bands, but of this there is no proof, except the following passage to be found in **Altowan,** a romantic novel based on his experiences:

> On the banks of a small stream, which ultimately finds its way into the upper waters of Snake River, a rugged path, made by the bison descending from a pass above, winds its way through the dwarf willows and quaking asp that line its side . . . on a sudden turn of the road round a projecting cliff, Altowan stopped to contemplate the scene below, which, though not new to him, is one of undying wonder and magnificence. Far over an extensive vale rise 'the three Tetons,' high above surrounding mountains; their peaked heads shine white against the azure sky, while other ranges succeed each other like waves beyond and beyond, until they merge into the purple haze of the Western Horizon.

By 1838, competition for beaver pelts was beginning to exhaust the streams, and the law of diminishing returns was making itself felt in the Rocky Mountain fur trade. Nevertheless, after the rendezvous of that year, the field commanders of the company assembled their trappers for another invasion of the Jackson's Hole country. Again Osborne Russell illuminates the scene:

> I started, with about thirty trappers, up Wind River, expecting the camp to follow in a few days. During our stay at the rendezvous it was rumored among the men that the company intended to bring no more supplies to the Rocky Mountains, and discontinue all further operations. This caused a great deal of discontent among the trappers and numbers left the party. 21st—We traveled up Wind River about thirty miles and encamped. 22nd—Continued up the river till noon, then left it to our right, traveled over a high ridge covered with pines, in a westerly direction about fifteen miles, and fell on to the Grosvent Fork. Next day we traveled about twenty miles down Grosvent Fork. 24th—Myself and another crossed the mountain in a northwest direction, fell on to a stream running into Lewis Fork, about ten miles below Jackson's Lake. Here we staid and trapped until the 29th. Then we started back to the Grosvent Fork, where we found the camp, consisting of about sixty men, under the direction of Mr. Dripps, with James Bridger pilot.

The next day the camp followed down the Grosvent
Fork to Jackson's Hole. In the meantime myself and
comrade returned to our traps, which we raised, and took
over the mountain in a southwest direction and overtook
the camp on Lewis Fork. The whole company was starving. Fortunately I had killed a deer in crossing the mountain, which made supper for the whole camp. Aug. 1st—
We crossed Lewis Fork and encamped and staid the next
day. 3d.—Camp crossed the mountain to Pierre's Hole and
the day following I started with my former comrade to
hunt beaver on the streams which ran from the Yellowstone. . . .

Trapper train in Teton Pass.

Russell's side trip appears to have been made cross
country from near the Cottonwood Creek tributary of the
Gros Ventre over the foothills of Mt. Leidy to Spread Creek,
where he set traps, then back along this same route to
Bridger's camp on the Gros Ventre, then back to Spread
Creek, and later down the Snake River, rejoining the main
camp near the mouth of the Gros Ventre. Russell's account
of the main expedition fits in very well with the brief entry
in Newell's diary—"up Wind River into Jackson's Hole, on
to Pier's Hole." Another trapper present was young Jim
Baker, famous Wyoming pioneer, who was making his first
visit to the mountains.

An entry in Russell's journal indicates that a party of trappers from Fort Hall reached Yellowstone Lake in 1838. Meek alleges that he went alone to Gardner's Hole after the rendezvous and later to Burnt Hole, the neighborhood of Hebgen Lake. Here he left a joking message on a buffalo skull.

Some evidence of wintering in Jackson's Hole is given by Robert Newell:

> Capt. Drips left in December for Wind River with his camp. Capt. Walker remained on Green River with a small party, where we are now. Snow about one foot. January 26, 1839, buffalow scarce. I spent last Christmas in Jackson's Hole. We spent the balance of the winter down on Green River, over on Ham's Fork, the spring commencing to open the first of March, 1839.

Kit Carson writes:

> On the return of Spring we commenced our hunt, trapped the tributaries of the Missouri to the head of Lewis Fork, and then started for the rendezvous on Green River, near the mouth of Horse Creek. . . .

In March, Meek, after wintering among the Nez Perces on the Salmon River, and acquiring an Indian wife (apparently his third), set out trapping again with a comrade named Allen to whom he was much attached.

> They traveled along up and down the Salmon, to Godin's River, Henry's Fork of the Snake, to Pierre's Fork, and Lewis' Fork, and the Muddy, and finally set their traps on a little stream that runs out of the pass which leads to Pierre's Hole.

Correlated with other data, the "pass which leads to Pierre's Hole" sounds very much like Teton Pass. Here, according to Victor, a horrible event occurred. Ambushed by Blackfeet, Meek managed to escape in a thicket, but the hapless Allen was caught, shot, and then gleefully dismembered within sight and sound of his companion. Meek is supposed to have wriggled away during the night and, "after twenty-six days of solitary and cautious travel," escaped to the place of rendezvous.

Information on the rendezvous of 1839 has survived through the account of F. A. Wislizenus, a German doctor and political refugee, who accompanied the St. Louis supply train in the interests of curiosity and recreation. In addition to offering a vivid picture of proceedings at the rendezvous, he also coments on the decline of the fur trade in the Rocky Mountains. Wislizenus, Ermatinger of the Hudson's Bay Company, the Munger-Griffin missionary party, and several hundred Indians left the rendezvous for Fort Hall, going by the Bear River route, which was soon to become a part of the Oregon Trail. As for the trappers, it appears that some of them, yielding to fate, disbanded, but Meek and Newell were among those who went to Fort Hall and later trapped around Brown's Hole (a valley made by the Green River along the northern base of the Uinta Range). Others were still attracted to Jackson's Hole, the heart of the prime beaver country. An eminent pioneer of Montana, W. T. Hamilton, got it from "old-timers" that:

> In the year 1839 a party of forty men started on an expedition up the Snake River. In the party were Ducharme, Louis Anderson, Jim and John Baker, Joe Power,

Free trapper under attack by Indians.

Skinning beaver in Jackson's Hole.

L'Humphrie, and others. They passed Jackson's Lake, catching many beaver, and crossed the Continental Divide, following down the Upper Yellowstone—Elk—River to the Yellowstone Lake.

This party was attacked by the Blackfeet near the outlet of Yellowstone Lake, suffering a loss of five men. The survivors, while trapping the Park, witnessed "Sulphur Mountain," the Mud Volcano, Yellowstone Falls at the head of the Canyon, and the pyrotechnic displays of "Fire Hole Basin."

Early in 1839, Russell hunted mountain sheep and trapped beaver along the Snake River below Jackson's Hole, returning to Fort Hall in June. Making up a party of four for the purpose of trapping in the Yellowstone and Wind River Mountains, he spent the Fourth of July at the outlet of Jackson Lake, near present Moran, then followed the Snake River northward to Lewis Lake and Shoshone Lake. The Shoshone Geyser Basin is described by Russell in meticulous detail, including the rhythmic "Hour Spring" which resembles present Union Geyser. From here they crossed over to Hayden Valley via the Midway Geyser Basin, there noting a "boiling lake" of deep indigo blue, about three hundred feet in diameter, probably the present Grand Prismatic Spring. After an extended camp at the outlet of Yellowstone Lake they went east to the head of Clark's Fork, thence back to the Yellowstone at the ford near Tower Falls, thence to Gardner's Hole and back to the lake outlet. En route they saw disturbing evidence of "a village of 300 or 400 lodges of Blackfeet" that had only recently been evacuated. In their camp on Pelican Creek, just east of the present Fishing Bridge campground, they were suddenly assailed by a horde of "70 or 80" Blackfeet "who rent the air with their horrid yells" and inflicted severe arrow wounds on Russell and one other. They fought off the Indians with their rifles, but suffered great pain and hardship in making their way back to Fort Hall via West Thumb, Snake River, Berry Creek and Conant Pass at the north end of the Teton Range. This was Russell's final sorrowful exit from Wonderland.

Two slim and shaky clues to other Yellowstone expeditions in the late 1830's are available. In his journal of 1839, while sojourning in the Utah country, apprentice trapper E. Willard Smith reports: "The country around the headwaters of the Yellowstone, a tributary of the Missouri, abounds in natural curiosities. There are volcanoes, volcanic productions and carbonated springs. Mr. Vasquez told me that he went to the top of one of these volcanoes, the crater of which was filled with pure water, forming quite a large lake." In his **Life in the Far West** (1849), a fictionalized account of the mountain men, with whom he had personally consorted in 1846, Lieutenant Ruxton tells how, on one occasion, Old Bill Williams, "tough as the parfleche soles of his moccasins," led seven of his hardy associates into a little-known region, beckoned thence by "a lofty peak" which fits the description of the Grand Tetons, entering "the valley lying about the lakes now called Eustis and Biddle, in which are many thermal and mineral springs, well known to the trappers by the name of Soda, Beer, and Brimstone Springs, and regarded by them with no little awe and curiosity, as being the breathing places of his Satanic majesty."

The year 1840 can be said to mark the formal demise of the Rocky Mountain fur trade, for in that year was held the fifteenth and last of these great conclaves of the wilderness, the trapper's rendezvous on Horse Creek of the Green River. It also marks the end of an epoch in the history of Jackson's Hole. The main chronicler of this fateful year was the Belgian, Pierre-Jean De Smet, a Jesuit priest who accompanied the American Fur Company's last expedition to the mountains so that he might survey the prospects for a Catholic mission among the Flathead Indians. This was the beginning of a series of epic pilgrimages to the Far West which were to make him one of the dominant figures in American frontier history. Andrew Drips headed the supply train. Also present were several Protestant missionaries and "the first avowed Oregon emigrant," Joel P. Walker, and his wife and five children. On April 30, the caravan left Westport, Missouri, and, after two months of traveling over the Great Plains in the midst of vast buffalo herds, it reached its destination. Writes Father De Smet:

> On the 30th [June] I came to the rendezvous, where a band of Flatheads, who had been notified of my coming, were already waiting for me. . . . On the 4th of July, I resumed my travels, with my Flatheads; ten brave Canadians also chose to accompany me. . . .

> Three days we ascended Green river, and one the 8th we crossed it, heading for an elevated plain which separates the waters of the Colorado from those of the Columbia. . . . On leaving this plain, we descended several thousand feet by a trail and arrived in Jackson's Hole [Jackson's Little Hole]. . . . Thence we passed into a narrow and extremely dangerous defile, which was at the same time picturesque and sublime. . . .

> On the 10th, after crossing the lofty mountain, we arrived upon the banks of Henry's Fork [Snake River], one of the principal tributaries of Snake [Columbia] river. The mass of snow melted during the July heat had swollen this torrent to a prodigious height. Its roaring waters rushed furiously down and whitened with their foam the great blocks of granite which vainly disputed the passage with them. The sight intimidated neither our Indians nor our Canadians; accustomed to perils of this sort, they rushed into the torrent on horseback and swam it. I dared not venture to do likewise. To get me over, they made a kind of sack of my skin tent; then they put all my things in and set me on top of it. The three Flatheads who had jumped in to guide my frail bark by swimming, told me, laughing, not to be afraid, that I was on an excellent boat.

73

And in fact this machine floated on the water like a majestic swan; and in less than ten minutes I found myself on the other bank, where we encamped for the night.

The next day we had another high mountain to climb [Teton Pass] through a thick pine forest, and at the top we found snow, which had fallen in the night to the depth of two feet.

Joe Meek relates that,

about the last of June . . . he started for the old rendezvous places of the American Companies, hoping to find some divisions of them at least, on the familiar camping ground. But his journey was in vain. Neither on Green River or Wind River, where for ten years he had been accustomed to meet the leaders and their men, his old comrades in danger, did he find a wandering brigade even. The glory of the American companies was departed, and he found himself solitary among his long familiar haunts.

However, this sad story does not fit in with De Smet's account nor with the testimony of Meek's own good friend, Robert Newell, who in June 1840 also left Fort Hall for the rendezvous:

Mr. Ermatinger arrived 13th of June. I went to the American rendezvous, Mr. Drips, Freab and Bridger from St. Louis with goods, but times were certainly hard, no beever, and everything dull. Some missionaries came along with them for the Columbia, Messrs. Clark, Smith, Littlejohn. I engaged to pilot them over the mountains, with their wagons and such used in crossing, to Fort Hall. There I bought their wagons. . . .

Unless Meek's memory was at fault, the discrepancy can only be explained on the assumption that Meek, approaching Green River by way of Jackson's Hole, simply did not look hard enough. Be that as it may, Meek avers that after his disappointed return to Fort Hall,

he set out on what proved to be his last trapping expedition, with a Frenchman, named Mattileau. They visited the old trapping grounds on Pierre's Fork, Lewis' Lake, Jackson's [Hoback] River, Jackson's Hole, Lewis River and Salt River: but beaver were scarce; and it was with a feeling of relief that, on returning by way of Bear River, Meek heard from a Frenchman whom he met there, that he was wanted at Fort Hall, by his friend Newell, who had something to propose to him.

74

What Newell had to propose to Meek was something revolutionary. On one of Newell's wagons Meek loaded his traps and his Indian family, and together they performed the historic feat of taking the first wagons through to the Columbia River. Their departure best symbolizes the death of the Rocky Mountain fur trade and the birth of the Oregon Trail. After Meek's visit in 1840, Jackson's Hole relapsed into virgin solitude. For twenty years thereafter there is little positive evidence of white men in this valley. It was forty-five years before the arrival of the first permanent settler. For over a hundred years the historic importance of Jackson's Hole as the continental crossroads of the Western fur trade has been all but forgotten.

Rocky Mountain men setting traps.

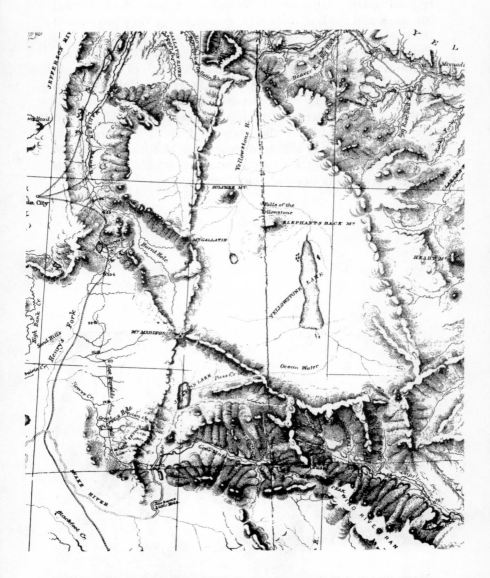

Section of Map accompanying *Report on the Exploration of the Yellowstone River*, by Bvt. Brig. Gen. W. F. Raynolds, Washington, 1868. Errors and omissions reflect failure of the Raynolds expedition to reach the Yellowstone Park area in 1860.

VIII. Epilogue: 1841-1870

After 1840 Yellowstone Park was likewise virtually left in primeval solitude. There is tangible evidence of only four visits of white men during this period, and one attempted visit which failed. In his recently published biography, William Clark Kennerly has it that in 1843 a grand hunting expedition headed by Sir William Drummond Stewart, and including such notables as Sublette and Baptiste Charbonneau, camped one evening among the geysers, having particularly great sport in vain efforts to throttle "old Steam Boat." In 1844, according to Chittenden, a party of trappers, identity not disclosed, entered Upper Yellowstone Valley from the south, and "passed around the west shore of Yellowstone Lake to the outlet, where they had a severe battle with the Blackfoot Indians, in a broad open tract at that point. The remains of their old corral were still visible as late as 1870." (This might be a variant of the same battle of 1939, told by Hamilton.)

The remaining three expeditions were guided by James Bridger, who in 1843 had set up Fort Bridger on Black's Fork of Green River, to cater to the emigrants who were beginning to follow the Oregon Trail. James Gemmell claims to have been among those present in 1846 when Bridger led "a trading expedition to the Crows and Sioux," north up the Green River through Jackson's Hole to West

Thumb, making a tour of the "wonderful spouting springs" and other scenic features before continuing down the Yellowstone. E. S. Topping states that in 1850 Jim Bridger, Kit Carson, and twenty-two others on a prospecting trip out of St. Louis "crossed the mountains to the Yellowstone and down it to the lake and the falls; then across the Divide to the Madison River. They saw the geysers of the lower basin and named the river that drains them the Fire Hole. . . . The report of this party made quite a stir in St. Louis."

The only historically discernible "stir" made by Bridger's reports consisted of the usual incredulity and scoffing, exemplified by the timidity of a Kansas City editor who in 1856 let immortality slip through his grasp by refusing to publish Bridger's own version of "the place where Hell bubbled up." By this time, however, one notable Bridger story had actually broken through the literary overcast, and two more would soon appear to vindicate the famous trapper. In 1852 Lieutenant Gunnison, who had been a member of the Howard Stansbury exploring party which Bridger guided to Great Salt Lake in 1849, published a romantic but essentially accurate description of the principal scenic features. Here is a "lake, sixty miles long," a "perpendicular canyon," the "Great Springs" on successive terraces, and "geysers spouting seventy feet high." In his letter mentioned above, published in 1863, constituting a report on his participation in the Fort Laramie treaty council of 1851, Father De Smet located what is substantially the present Park "in the very heart of the Rocky Mountains, between the 43d and 45th degrees of latitude, and the 109th and 111th degrees of longitude; that is between the sources of the Madison and the Yellowstone," regarding it as "the most marvellous spot of all the northern half of the continent" because of its boiling springs, calcareous hills, escaping vapors, steamboat noises, subterranean explosions and, near Gardner River, " a mountain of sulphur." In this case likewise the source of his information was Bridger, "who is familiar with every one of these mounds, having passed thirty years of his life near them."

Even more illuminating to the historian than the well-known De Smet letter are five unpublished maps traced by that missionary. These maps had little contemporary influence and, though noted by his biographers in 1905, they have been neglected by subsequent historians. They are documents of signal import, which should inspire renewed respect for the ubiquitous Bridger and yet increase the stature of the versatile and indefatigable De Smet, already one of the giants of western history. Of these five maps four are still at St. Louis University, which was his headquarters. These are among dozens which were made by him in the course of his several western journeys, the information obtained by acute personal observation as well as "from trappers and intelligent Indians." The draftsmanship of the first three, while not striking, is respectable. One shows "Yellow Stone" River and tributaries as high as "Gardner's F." A second, embracing the Upper Missouri, Yellowstone, and Upper Platte regions, shows a nameless bladder-shaped lake at the head of the Yellowstone and a conspicuous "Hot Sulphur Spring" north of the lake. A third, embracing the entire West from the Great Basin to the Forks of the Platte, shows essentially the same features. The fourth map in the St. Louis collection is the most intriguing. This depicts that remarkable twisted region of the Rocky Mountains where the headwaters of the Yellowstone, the Wind, the Green, the Snake, and the Missouri rivers unwind before rolling to their respective oceans. The undated map is crude and smeary, and it has all the earmarks of being sketched in the field without benefit of desk or blotter. In view of De Smet's express testimony that the most famous trapper of all supplied him with his geographic data, at least for the "Yellowstone Park" section, it is a fair guess that this was drawn by De Smet with Bridger at his elbow. Here, on a rough chart consigned to the oblivion of a library vault, is where "Yellowstone Park" first comes into clear focus. Allowing for pardonable distortions, all of the principal scenic features are in evidence: the geyser basins of the Firehole ("volcanic country"); Mammoth Hot Springs ("Sulphur Mountain" near "Gardener's Cr."); a shapeless Yellowstone Lake ("60 by 9") with "Hot

79

Springs" and "Great Volcanoes" alongside; the Grand Canyon and "Falls 290 feet"; and Hayden Valley ("Volcanic country [?] Steam Springs"). Two Ocean Pass, Jackson Lake, and "Colter's Hell" on Stinking River are other conspicuous features near by.

The "Bridger Map" is the obvious source of the Yellowstone data found on the fifth De Smet map, embracing the western United States, which is more carefully drawn than the others. This large untitled map, with a bold floral border, is dated 1851, and contains the following fading inscription within curved palm fronds: "respectfully presented to Col. David D. [?] Mitchell [by] P. J. De Smet, Soc. Jes." As to the circumstances under which this map was drawn, De Smet explains as follows in a letter dated July 1, 1857, to officials of the Department of the Interior:

> When I was at the council ground in 1851, on the Platte River, at the mouth of the Horse creek, I was requested by Colonel Mitchell [superintendent of Indian Affairs at St. Louis] to make a map of the whole Indian country, relating particularly to the Upper Missouri, the waters of the upper Platte, east of the Rocky mountains and of the headwaters of the Columbia and its tributaries west of these mountains. In compliance with this request I drew up the map from scraps then in my possession. The map, so prepared, was seemingly approved and made use of by the gentlemen assembled in council, and subsequently sent on to Washington together with the treaty then made with the Indians. In my humble opinion, therefore, it can be of very little service for your purposes, in which accuracy of instrumental measurements and observation seems to be absolutely necessary. . . .

The final gesture of modesty may explain why this revealing map, prepared and made available to the government twenty years before the first official Park exploration got under way, was duly glanced at by the department authorities and then tucked away, a needle in the haystack of official files, in Washington, D. C., where it still reposes. It contains all the features of the "Bridger Map," but with refinements. Here is a "Great Volcanic Region [?] now in a state of eruption," drained by "Fire Hole Riv." The lake now appear as "Yellowstone or Sublette's Lake," still oddly sausage-shaped. There is a "Little Falls" at the head of the canyon but the more impressive Lower Falls are unexplainably omitted. To the southwest, in the position of present Shoshone Lake, is "De Smet Lake." To the east at the forks of "Stinking Fr." appears the "Sulphur Springs or Colter's Hell Volcano" which, due to the unavailability of this map, has led so many historians astray. This map, with its manuscript forebears, ranks with the Ferris journal and map and the Potts letter as one of the principal historical documents pertaining to early Yellowstone.

It is not evident that information given by Gunnison and De Smet or any of their predecessors relative to unusual phenomena on the Upper Yellowstone greatly impressed representatives of the Federal Government. Certainly no eagerness to verify these reports is betrayed in the official instructions dated April 13, 1859, by which Captain Raynolds, Corps of Topographical Engineers, was directed "to organize an expedition for the exploration of the region of the country through which flow the principal tributaries of the Yellowstone river, and of the mountains in which they, and the Gallatin and Madison forks of the Missouri, have their source." However, since one of the objects of this exploration was to ascertain the principal topographical features and since, moreover, the indispens-

Trappers in Pierre's Hole, west of "Les Trois Tetons"

able Bridger was secured as a guide, it would seem that the Yellowstone marvels were just about to be officially discovered and proclaimed. Not so, however. The expedition left winter camp on Platte River in May 1860. While a detachment under Lieutenant Henry E. Maynadier went north along the eastern slope of the Absaroka Range, the main party ascended Wind River to Union Pass, then turned north seeking the headwaters of the Yellowstone. Deep snow and a great "basaltic ridge" blocked their efforts before they reached Two Ocean Pass, and they had to satisfy themselves with encircling the Park area via Jackson's Hole, Teton Pass, Henry's Fork, and Raynolds' Pass. By way of the Madison, they rejoined Maynadier at the Three Forks. Raynolds' report and map became the first recognition by the Federal Government of the possible existence of volcanic activity in the region of the Upper Yellowstone. For information regarding the "burning plains, immense lakes, and boiling springs" and other unverifiable phenomena mentioned he was, of course, indebted to his guide Bridger, with trimmings added by Meldrum. On his "Map of the Yellowstone and Missouri Rivers," within the "enchanted enclosure" which now constitutes Yellowstone National Park, the soldier-explorer had the courage to place "Yellowstone Lake," "Falls of the Yellowstone," "Burnt Hole," "Sulphur Mountain," and "Elephant's Back Mt.," all now recognizable features. This was an extraordinary demonstration of faith in Bridgers veracity. Because of the Civil War, publication of the report was delayed until 1868, but the map itself was first issued separately a few years earlier.

It was the discovery of gold, first in California and later in Colorado, which started the population moving centrally westward in great numbers and diverted whatever attention might otherwise have become focussed on the Upper Yelowstone region. It was the discovery of gold in western Montana which brought about its rediscovery and early creation as the world's first National Park. Although there was desultory prospecting previous to 1862, it was in that year that the news of several major gold strikes was broadcast and a full scale stampede to the diggings began.

In the spring of 1863 at least two prospecting parties entered the Park. Although they were feverishly preoccupied with the search for gold, the unusual character of the country did not escape them entirely, and the leader of one party made something akin to the first scientific eyewitness report. This was Walter W. DeLacy, a professional surveyor. In August 1863 he fell in with an expedition of forty-two men bound for Snake River, and was elected captain. Their search being unrewarded, fifteen of the party deserted at Jackson Lake, the others deciding to push north. From the junction of the Lewis and the Snake they went over the Pitchstone Plateau to discover Shoshone Lake and Lewis Lake. From there they crossed over the Divide to the geyser basins of the Firehole. Although amazed at the "Steamboat Springs" they had little time for sight-seeing, and left the Park by way of the Gallatin. DeLacy's discoveries were incorporated in his "Map of the Territory of Montana," which was published "for the use of the First Legislature of Montana" in 1865. His accurate firsthand knowledge of the western section of the Park is reflected in the correct relationship of "Jackson's Lake" and unnamed Lewis Lake and Shoshone Lake, and in the "Hot Spring Valley" or geyser basin at the headwaters of the Madison. Identifiable features of the unvisited eastern section consist only of a misshapen "Yellow Stone Lake" and the "Falls."

We have recognized the Ferris map of 1836 and the De Smet map of 1851, based on the undated "Bridger Map," as the earliest authentic maps of the Yellowstone Park area, but these remained unpublished and unheralded. The Raynolds and DeLacy maps, though purporting to reveal the scenic wonders, were scanned mainly by single-minded gold seekers before they became obsolete. As to other contemporary published maps, the persistence of this geographical blind spot in the face of testimony offered by such prime witnesses as Potts, Ferris, and Bridger is demonstrated by the fact that for over half a century of map making by such respected cartographers are John Arrowsmith, Albert Gallatin, Bonneville, Fremont, and Gouverneur K. Warren there was no improvement in the "Yellowstone Park" section of the Clark map of 1810, with its "Lake Eustis" and "Hot Spring Brimstone." There were only occasional meaningless variations of nomenclature. For instance, on the Robert Greenhow map of 1840 and on E. F. Beade's "New Map of the Great West," published in 1856, "Hot Sulphur Springs" is substituted. On Charles Wilkes' "Map of Oregon Territory" which appeared in 1845 and on the J. H. Colton map which accompanied **Horn's Overland Guide,** published in 1856, this phenomenon becomes "Steamboat Sp." and Eustis is transformed into "Sublette's L." However, on the famed Colton map of 1867, just five years before the first boat was launched from its shores, the phantom lake—Eustis Sublette, or Yellowstone—has disappeared entirely!

Contemporary newspaper accounts and later published reminiscences reveal several prospecting expeditions which traversed the Park area during the period 1864-1869, but the partial and foggy reports of "a lost world" given out by these treasure hunters did little to dispel the curtain of mystery stubbornly surrounding the area. The cumulative effect of such reports and rumors, however, was destined soon to convince intelligent listeners that no wild tale could be so persistent, and that there must be something at the headwaters of the Yellowstone worth looking into. In September 1869, David E. Folsom, Charles W. Cook, and William Peterson packed south out of Diamond City, Montana, without distracting thoughts of beaver hides or gold, but with the express purpose of exploring that neighborhood and reporting their findings without adornment. General Henry D. Washburn, Hon. Cornelius Hedges, Hon. Nathaniel Langford, Dr. Ferdinand V. Hayden, and Photographer William H. Jackson were standing in the wings. The brief era of definitive discovery was dawning.

First picture ever made of Yellowstone Lake from watercolor
by Henry W. Elliott, 1871.

Picture courtesy of Haynes Studios, Inc.

Selected Bibliography for

COLTER'S HELL AND JACKSON'S HOLE

Allen, Paul, *History of the Expedition Under the Command of Captains Lewis and Clark*, 2 vols. (Philadelphia, 1814).

Alter, J. Cecil, *James Bridger* (Salt Lake City, 1925).

Bancroft, H. H., *History of Nevada, Colorado and Wyoming, 1540-1888* (San Francisco, 1890).

Barry, J. Neilson (ed.), "Journal of E. Willard Smith," *Quarterly of the Oregon Historical Society* (September 1913).

Bonneville, Captain B. L. E., undated letter from Fort Smith, Arkansas, *Contributions to the Historical Society of Montana* (Helena), I (1876), 93-97.

Brackenridge, Henry M., *Views of Louisiana* (Pittsburgh, 1814).

Bradbury, John, *Travels in the Interior of North America, 1809-1811* (London, 1819), republished in Reuben G. Thwaites (ed.), *Early Western Travels*, 32 vols. (Cleveland, 1904-1907), V.

Burpee, Lawrence J. (ed.), *Journal of Larocque from the Assiniboine to the Yellowstone, 1805* (Ottawa, 1910).

Carter, Clarence E. (ed.), *Territorial Papers of the United States* (Washington, 1934, XIII, *Territory of Louisiana-Missouri, 1803-1806* (1948).

Chittenden, Hiram M., *The American Fur Trade of the Far West*, 2 vols., ed. by Stallo Vinton (New York, 1936).

Chittenden, Hiram M. and Richardson, Albert T., *Life, Letters and Travels of Father Pierre-Jean De Smet, S. J., 1801-1873* (New York, 1905), 4 vols.

Chittenden, Hiram M., *The Yellowstone National Park, Historical and Descriptive* (Cincinnati, 1895).

Coues, Elliott (ed.), *Forty Years a Fur Trader . . . Charles Larpenteur*, 2 vols. (New York, 1898).

Coutant, Charles G., *History of Wyoming* (Laramie, 1899).

Dale, Harrison C., *The Ashley-Smith Explorations* (Glendale, 1941).

DeLacy, Walter W., *Map of the Territory of Montana, etc.* (St. Louis, 1865).

DeLacy, Walter W., "A Trip Up the South Snake River in 1863," *Contributions to the Historical Society of Montana*, I (1876).

De Smet, Pierre Jean, *Western Missions and Missionaries* (New York, 1863).

DeVoto, Bernard, *Across the Wide Missouri* (Boston, 1947).

DeVoto, Bernard (ed.), *Life and Adventures of James P. Beckwourth* (New York, 1931).

Ellison, William H., *Life and Adventures of George Nidever* (Berkeley, 1937).

Frost, Donald M., *Notes on General Ashley, the Overland Trail and South Pass* (Worcester, 1944).

Grant, Blanche C. (ed.), *Kit Carson's Own Life Story* (Taos, 1926).

Gunnison, John W., *The Mormons, or Latter-Day Saints in the Valley of the Great Salt Lake* (Philadelphia, 1852).

Hamilton, William T., *My Sixty Years on the Plains* (New York, 1905).

Harris, Burton, *John Colter, His Years in the Rockies* (New York, 1952).

Irving, Washington, *Astoria, or Anecdotes of an Enterprise Beyond the Rocky Mountains,* 3 vols. (Philadephia, 1836).

Irving, Washington, *The Rocky Mountains . . . The Journal of Captain B. L. E. Bonneville,* 2 vols. (Philadelphia, 1837).

James, Thomas, *Three Years Among the Indians,* ed. by Walter B. Douglas (St. Louis, 1916), reprinted from original edition of 1846.

Kennerly, William C., *Persimmon Hill: A Narrative of Old St. Louis* (Norman, 1948).

Laut, Agnes, *Conquest of the Great Northwest* (G. H. Doran Co., 1908).

Lindsay, Charles, *The Big Horn Basin* (Lincoln, 1932).

Mattes, Merrill J., "Behind the Legend of Colter's Hell: The Early Exploration of Yellowstone National Park," *Mississippi Valley Historical Review* (September 1949).

Mattes, Merrill J., "Jackson Hole, Crossroads of the Western Fur Trade, 1807-1840," *Pacific Northwest Quarterly* (April 1946 and January 1948).

Parker, Samuel, *Journal of an Exploring Tour Beyond the Rocky Mountains* (Ithaca, 1944).

Phillips, Paul C. (ed.), *Life in the Rocky Mountains; A Diary . . . by Warren A. Ferris* (Denver, 1940).

Potts, Daniel T., Letters, *Yellowstone Nature Notes* (September 1947).

Raynolds, General William F., "Report on the Explorations of the Yellowstone River" (Washington, 1868), *Senate Executive Documents,* No. 77. 40 Cong. 1 [2] Sess.

Rollins, Philip A. (ed.), *The Discovery of the Oregon Trail* (Hunt and Stuart Journals) (New York, 1935).

Ross, Alexander, *The Fur Hunters of the Far West,* 2 vols. (London, 1855).

Russell, Osborne, *Journal of a Trapper,* edited by Aubrey L. Haines (Portland, 1955).

Sabin, Edwin L., *Kit Carson Days,* 2 vols. (New York, 1935).

Sullivan, M. S., *Travels of Jedediah Smith* (Santa Ana, 1934).

Thwaites, Reuben G., *Oregon; or, a Short History . . . by John B. Wyeth (Early Western Travels)* (Cleveland, 1905), XXI.

Thwaites, Reuben G. (ed.), *Original Journals of the Lewis and Clark Expedition 1804-1806,* 8 vols. (New York, 1904-1905), V.

Topping, E. S., *Chronicles of the Yellowstone* (St. Paul, 1883).

Victor, Frances Fuller, *The River of the West* (Hartford, 1870).

Vinton, Stallo, *John Colter, Discoverer of Yellowstone Park* (New York, 1926).

Wagner, W. F. (ed.), *Leonard's Narrative; Adventures of Zenas Leonard 1831-1836* (Cleveland, 1904).

Webb, J. Watson (ed.), *Altowan,* 2 vols. (New York, 1846).

Wislizenus, F. A., *A Journey to the Rocky Mountains in 1839* (St. Louis, 1912).